COUNT SAINT GERMAIN

The New Age Prophet Who Lives Forever

Arthur Crockett &
Timothy Green Beckley

With Special Channelings from the Master
through William Alexander Oribello

Editorial Direction & Layout
Timothy Green Beckley

Manuscript Production
Gene Steinberg

Copyright © 1984 & 2002
by Tim Beckley dba Inner Light
All Rights Reserved
ISBN: 1-892062-20-8

No part of this book may be reproduced, stored in a retrieval system or transmitted, in any form or by any means. electronic, mechanical, photocopying, recording, or otherwise, without prior permission of the publisher. Manufactured in the United States of America.

**Special thanks to Carol Ann Rodriguez
and William Alexander Oribello**

Published by:
INNER LIGHT PUBLICATIONS
Box 753
New Brunswick, NJ 08903

You Can Be Your Own Alchemist & Discover The "Philosophers Stone!"

Students the world over have come to accept him as a true Ascended Master, as spiritually advanced as the Christ or Buddha. Many contend that he is still very much alive and is nearing his 400th birthday. He is said to reside in a hidden monastery in a city beneath Tibet, but can telepathically communicate, as well as materialize in physical form, to his faithful followers when they are troubled the most. Frequently, he offers healing prayers, and guidance to aid deserving souls in times of great personal needs.

Throughout the last four centuries, he has walked the Earth in a variety of disguises easily mingling with world leaders in order to promote the virtues of freedom and democracy. It is claimed that he remains especially fond of the United States, and actually worked with the founding fathers to draw up the Bill of Rights and the Declaration of Independence. Several times, he has supposedly saved this country from great harm by appearing before our President to offer advice and wisdom from the higher realms.

Among others, Napoleon was so taken with Saint Germain's activities in Europe that he had formed a special commission to investigate the life of this man to see if there was any truth to the many fantastic stories being widely spread about him. The commission's findings were destroyed in a fierce fire that is thought to be more than coincidence.

As the greatest of all alchemists, Saint Germain has not only turned metal into gold, but has mastered the secrets of eternal youth. Now the authors of this book conclude that Saint Germain's ability to never grow old lie not just in his metaphysical teachings, but in the proper diet, exercise and meditation. As we move further along into the New Age it is, they say, possible for each of us to accomplish much of what Saint Germain has achieved during his long life, to literally become our own alchemist and discover for ourselves the secrets of the Philosopher's Stone.

CONTENTS

A rare portrait of Count St. Germain commissioned in 1785 by the Marquise d'Urfe just months before St. Germain faked his own death.

Special Preface

by William Alexander Oribello,
Founder, Mystic Light Society

During the past hundred years, several books have appeared concerning Count St. Germain, the wonder man of the occult world; but none so simply presented as the book you are now reading. This work is a key that will unlock the door to higher dimensions of spiritual power and development.

While little is known of the origin of Count St. Germain, general history reveals that he was born about 1561, and died in 1784. But there are countless mysteries connected to this unique individual. For example, the inner circle of initiates know that he was probably born much earlier than records show, and all indications are that he never died. It is believed that he is one of those rare people, who had reached an advanced state of illumination to the degree of transmuting the physical body into higher vibration, so that it eventually became one with Spirit.

My personal experience with Count St. Germain began in my late teen years. I had not heard of him before this time. It was about a year before I began my public spiritual work. I was suddenly awakened one night to find three people in my room. These beings were dressed in the garb of the Three Wise Men of Biblical lore. They were the Ascended Masters Kuthumi, El Morya and Count St. Germain. A bright light surrounded their forms, and they showed me a great book filled with esoteric wisdom. They said that this knowledge and wisdom would be locked within my heart, and that when it was time, I would record much of it in my future writings.

Later, one of my teachers explained that the entity known as Count St. Germain had lived several lives since his grand initiation before the time of Christ, and that he had lived during the time of Christ. During the

5

dark ages, he lived again as a young genius and adept who came to a group of mystic monks, for the purpose of helping them preserve the tradition of Mystic Christianity which was vanishing amidst the rapid development of organized religion. In that life, he died at a young age, but in the next century he returned to establish a true fraternity of Light that still exists today, and works to preserve the secret doctrine. It is believed that he achieved the Grand Arcanum in that lifetime, whereby he overcame death itself and became a true master, working and living under many names.

In 1982 I had another encounter with Count St. Germain. He appeared in physical form and gave me several messages concerning my work. He made several predictions concerning the direction my work would take, including my eventual association with Inner Light Publications.

Count St. Germain has been an inspiration to aspiring adepts, including Count Cagliostro, founder of The Egyptian Rite of Freemasonry. The author of this book refers to the Secret Right of Immortality, taught to the inner circle of Count Cagliostro. Esoteric tradition reveals that Cagliostro learned this from Count St. Germain. At first glance, this rite seems to make little sense, and it would be foolish for anyone to take it literally. In reality, the rite is symbolic for a powerful esoteric formula to completely transform a person—morally and physically. It is time for this rite to be explained in a published work, that more students may benefit from the knowledge it conceals. Therefore, I will now present this rite as it was expounded in the outer teachings, followed by my explanation of its true meaning.

Those desiring to experience moral transmutation were taught to separate themselves from the world for forty days. During that time they were to spend six hours a day in contemplation; three hours in prayer; nine hours in the practices of the fraternity, and the balance of the day for rest. On the thirty-third day, the practitioner would receive communications from the seven primordial spirits, and on the fortieth day be reborn inwardly.

To achieve physical transmutation, the practitioner was instructed to retire to a secret place during the month of May, and remain on a strict fast for forty days. On the seventeenth day they are to draw blood and take a concoction known as 'white drops'. These are taken for three days, after which he draws blood from his arm, then takes a grain of 'philosopher's stone for three more days. After this, he experiences a series of convulsive physical hardships, during which he sheds his skin and loses his hair and teeth. These are all replaced within a few hours, and on the fortieth day, he is completely rejuvenated and may live 5,557 years if he so desires.

As stated earlier, this two–fold rite is symbolic for a powerful esoteric formula for personal transformation. For example, the first part teaches initiates to separate themselves from the world for forty days. This is symbolic of the initiate becoming aware of the four levels of being: physical, emotional, mental, and spiritual. In the Quabballistic Teachings, each level of being is divided into ten sub-levels termed 'the Tree of Life', thus four times ten equals forty. All who have attained an advanced degree of self-mastery have been said to study or seek 'the wilderness' (to make the special effort to learn their true nature) for forty days (or years). We can even find this allegory in the Holy Bible, in the accounts of the inner awakening of Moses, Elijah and Jesus Christ.

During the forty days, the initiate was instructed to spend six hours a day in contemplation. To understand the significance of number six, let us turn our attention to two Biblical Stories: the first is the Account of Creation. We are told that the Almighty Spirit created all things in six days. The second is the account of when Jesus had six pots filled with water and turned the water into wine. Both of these symbolic stories refer to the fact that the process of inner transformation is like the creation of a new person, and this process is associated with the number six in some occult teachings. As we contemplate our lives with its success & failures, good memories & regrets, ups and downs, we come to realize our purpose. We know where we come from and where we are going. We learn the valuable lessons of our mistakes inwardly, and this leads to inner awakening and development.

During the forty days, one is also advised to spend three hours a day in prayer. This is symbolic of refining and directing our physical, emotional and mental energies towards the reality of Spirit, to the best of our ability.

Nine hours a day spent in the practices of the fraternity is symbolic of a degree work in passing through the Nine Initiations of The Lesser Mysteries. All genuine wisdom schools present these initiations in one form or another.

The statement to the effect that on the thirty–third day, the practitioner would receive communications from the seven primordial spirits refers to wisdom school training in a three degree system: there are three degrees, with three initiations within each degree, making a total of nine initiations of the lesser mysteries. The mystic number 33 which appears in occult and religious teachings so often, refers to the formula 3 x 3 = 9. The seven primordial spirits refer to the seven etheric energy centers, known as 'chakras' which channel cosmic forces into our physical existence via the seven ductless glands. At another level the seven primordial spirits are symbolic of the energies that work through the seven planets recognized in magickal systems. We can, therefore, conclude that 'communications from the seven primordial spirits' means to get in touch with these energies.

The second part of the secret rite, implicating physical rejuvenation, informs the practitioner to retire to a secret place during the month of May and remain on a strict fast for forty days. In addition to the forty day symbolism which has already been considered, the Month of May has special significance. To understand this, it is necessary to consider a Pagan Festival of the Old Religion—that of the Bealtaine or May Day's Eve (April 30th). This festival celebrated the advent of the warm season, when people began to feel renewed in anticipation of the pleasures of summer. This is symbolic of the physical vitality or life-force. The fast is symbolic of conserving our physical energy during certain phases of intense metaphysical training.

On the seventeenth day, the initiate is instructed to draw blood and to take the 'white drops' for three days. If we reduce the number seventeen to a single digit we have, 1 + 7 = 8. Eight is the number of regeneration or a new beginning. The drawing of blood is not literal but symbolic: it is said "the life is in the blood". Adepts of the Mystic Path know a person's blood contains a 'cell consciousness' of ancestors, and even past lives. Some of this consciousness may restrict us in our quest for spiritual mastery. Through certain techniques of the Path, harmful cell consciousness is released and this is the real meaning of drawing blood.

The white drops mentioned in the rite has more than one level of reality: at one level, they are the result of materialization which takes place in the brain every month, termed "the Brain Dew". Instructions for the process of harnessing the power of the Brain Dew is given in genuine wisdom school training. At another level, the white drops are an actual potion of one part melted butter, two parts honey, and four parts coconut milk. Many sages have used this formula for increased vitality and magnetism.

The three days mentioned in the second part of the rite has the same significance as described in the first. It means to direct our physical, emotional and mental energies towards the reality of Spirit. Again, it mentions drawing blood, but it specifically mentions the arm, symbolic of restraining our aggressive expressions in daily life as much as possible.

After all this, the initiate is instructed to take a grain of the philosopher's stone every day for three more days, and prepare to experience convulsive physical hardships, during which they shed their skin, hair and teeth. Let us first explore the mysterious philosopher's stone.

The mystic alchemists, said to transmute base metal into gold, used a mysterious substance termed "The Philosopher's Stone". They created this from three ingredients of salt, sulphur and mercury, adding a fourth termed "Azoth" or the secret fire. Salt is symbolic of the physical part of our being, sulphur is symbolic of the emotional (astral) part of our being, and mercury is symbolic of the mental part of our being. The secret fire refers to calling forth the Power of Spirit to properly activate and use the spinal fire (also known by the Eastern term "Kundalini') with the guidance of a qualified wisdom school instructor. The philosopher's stone is within you.

Growing into higher levels of awareness causes a certain degree of upheaval in one's life: friends and loved ones not in agreement with this advanced knowledge, will begin to feel uncomfortable around the initiate (unless they seek the path to self improvement too), we are faced with the necessity to release many personal illusions, and this can be painful. Our emotions and thoughts will pass through several stages of change, and it is like melting all that we cherish in an imaginary furnace of fire, and reshaping it. Consider all the phases of breaking down and change that silver, gold and precious stones pass through to become a beautiful piece of jewelry. So is the initiate. We pass through many changes, but take comfort in the knowledge that we are becoming someone more beautiful and masterful in every way.

During this time of self-transformation, it is warned that the initiate's hair and teeth will fall out, and that he will shed his skin, but all of these will be replaced within a few hours. It has been said that a brave person has thick skin, and an overly sensitive person has a thin skin. Hair is symbolic of beauty or vanity. Teeth are symbolic of strength. This mysterious statement implies that the initiate reorganizes priorities, redirects their methods of self expression, and works to achieve a greater sense of harmony and balance. That all which was lost will be replaced in a few hours means that once we approach the Great Work correctly, we will become a new person in a short time.

It is further said that by the fortieth day, the initiate will be a completely new person, and may live 5,557 years if he so desires. $5 + 5 + 5 + 7 = 22$. Therefore this is an arcane figure, symbolic of the twenty-two paths of illumination, as illustrated in the twenty two cards of the Major Arcana of the Tarot. It means that the initiate has achieved the Great Work. However, let us keep in mind that while this rite is symbolic for the inner transformation, the results can be very real in physical life. Several adepts have taken the work so far as to actually extend their physical life to a great age. There is Babaji, who is about 2,000 years old, and Count St. Germain who is well over 300 years old. But I must add that when a person achieves this, there comes a time when they will not be able to live in daily society. Babaji lives in a hidden retreat in the Himalayas. Count St. Germain lives in a retreat of the Ascended Masters. Both of these Masters, as well as others like them, do appear in the everyday world when their assistance is needed by one of their initiates.

A never before seen photo of what could be the actual "Athanor" or "digesting furnace" used by St. Germain in his work as an alchemist.

Count St. Germain— The Man Who Lives Forever

You are probably aware of the fact that today man lives an average of three score and ten years. The Old Testament tells us that in Biblical days people lived as long as 800 and 900 years. Why the big difference? What did the spiritual leaders of ages past know about the longevity which we obviously have long since forgotten? Was it the way they lived? Was it due to the fact that they led spiritual lives, or were close with God? Perhaps it had to do with their diet and the purity of the air. Indeed, as we shall see, perhaps all these things helped account for their ability to live beyond the normal number of years that most of we mortals survive to.

Many different theories have been offered as to the reason certain sages and avatars live such a long time. We know for a fact that one man in modern times has obviously found the key to living a long, prosperous existence.

What's more, he still lives!

Far-fetched? Certainly, on the surface it would seem so. But if you follow this narrative to the end, you may have other thoughts. You may agree that the man in question is not only alive, but that you may even know who he is!

This book, therefore, is a chronological record of the man and his deeds. Further, it is an amazing tale of the one who is not likely to die... ever.

His name is Count St. Germain.

Who is Count St. Germain?

There are some who say he was born to Queen Elizabeth in 1561. Others contend he was the last of the Tudor family. The identity of his actual parents remains to this day a mystery, as does the man St. Germain himself. During his early years he is said to have become the adopted son of Lord and Lady Bacon who named him Frances Bacon. His writings have appeared under such names as Shakespeare, Christopher Marlowe, Spencer, Montaigne, Burton, Cervantes and others. After his feigned death in England, he appeared in Europe and continued to write under the names of Valentine Andraes, Comte de Bagalis and others. He used these names to conceal his real identity.

The man was definitely no myth. People well known in history and literature called him their friend. Frederick the Great, for instance, referred to Saint Germain as "the man who never dies." He was known personally to Voltaire, Rousseau, Walpole and Casanova. In the memoirs of Madame de Pompadour she tells of being lost in admiration of his charm and wide knowledge.

St. Germain was also the last heir to the house of Rakoczy in Transylvania and throughout the long history of this man he was never in want. He was always wealthy, always brilliant and eternally young. He regarded the crown heads of Europe as his equals. Royalty's private chambers were always open to him. He usually disappeared as mysteriously as he appeared, and his disappearances were marked by feigned deaths.

St. Germain The Prophet

This enigmatic man was a philosopher, poet and dramatist. On occasion he did make predictions which came true. Writers and other thinkers who knew him said that he had the power to see into the future; there is also evidence that he knew in advance his own destiny and his own accomplishments. A startling example was recorded by Franz Graeffer in his book, "Recollections of Vienna." St. Germain told the author: "Tomorrow night I am off; I am much needed in Constantinople, then in England, there to prepare two inventions which you will have in the next century—trains and steamboats."

St. Germain spoke these words in the 1700s, when trains and steamboats were still unknown in the world!

St. Germain's Prophecy of the French Revolution

In 1768, long before there was any thought of a revolt in France, St. Germain had so endeared himself to the throne that he was permitted unrestricted admittance into the royal private apartments. His wealth was a mystery, nor did anyone know where he acquired his magnificent jewels. But while they pondered those questions, St. Germain saw terror and bloodshed in France's future.

His vision was revealed in a book by Comtesse d'Adhemar titled, "Souvenirs sur Marie Antoinette." Here it was said that he wrote a poem to the queen:

The time draws near when France so imprudent will fall on misfortunes she could well have held off; She'll remember the Hell which Dante has painted: Oh, queen, have no doubts that day is at hand.

St. Germain also told of blood and tears and exile, civil war and strife, and many executions. The author of the memoirs states that St. Germain appointed a tryst for Madame d'Adhemar in the church of the Recollets, early in the morning, and in that place informed the author that the queen was doomed to die unless she heeded the warnings. He said the Revolution would be aimed at the complete destruction of the Bourbons.

They will appear from all the thrones they occupy and in less than a century they will return in their different branches to the rank of simple private persons. France as Kingdom, Republic, Empire and mixed government will be tormented, agitated, torn apart. From the hands of class tyrants she will pass to those who are ambitious and without merit.

Some of St. Germain's Accomplishments

The man known as St. Germain, also Saint Germain, Count de Saint Germain, and Comte de St. Germain, was master of all European languages, and spoke them without accent. He was one of the best swordsmen in the world and his technique with a violin was equalled only by Paganini.

He was able to write two different letters at the same time, using both hands. Each was an exact copy of the other to such an extent that when one was placed on top of the other and held up to a light they were found to be identical right down to the last detail!

Saint Germain had a photographic memory which enabled him to repeat word for word the entire contents of a newspaper even though several days had passed.

The man was adept at the "single-glance" technique, meaning he was able to walk swiftly through a room and take in so much information about the contents and people present that it would require someone hours of writing to record everything he saw. It was possible for him to absorb the entire contents of a letter someone was reading in a chair nearby.

This technique is not exclusive with St. Germain. The Japanese and the Russians trained their spies in World War II to develop a sort of "picture holding" technique. And the practice is still adhered to in espionage circles. However, no one was as adept at it as St. Germain.

His Greatest Accomplishment—Living Forever

Cagliostro was a disciple of St. Germain, who taught him the alchemical art. Cagliostro also learned from the master the Secret Rite of Longevity, and in fact used the rejuvenating elixir on aging individuals to restore their youth. We must assume then that St. Germain himself practiced the Secret Rite to insure his own longevity.

The Secret Rite

The strange operation consisted of a 40-day fast, during which only distilled water was used, plus an elixir called the "Master's White Drops."

On the thirty-third day, the individual on the fast would experience an evacuation from all channels of the body. That would be accompanied by great perspiration. On the thirty-fifth day, one's hair and teeth would fall out. The skin would be shed. On the thirty-seventh day, new skin would form and new teeth start to grow. By the fortieth day, a complete rejuvenation would be accomplished.

The theory is that if one repeats this process every 50 years, one's physical immortality will be secured.

The Indian sage, Mahatma Ghandi, had this treatment recommended to him. The Ayuvedic method, similar to the Cagliostro Secret Rite, was practiced in India for thousands of years, and is supposed to treat disease and restore health.

Ghandi never tried the treatment. One of his followers did. It was successful. The one who applied the treatment was a yogi 178 years old. He looked no more than 40.

The Ayuvedic school of medicine also insists on a 40-day fast to dissolve accumulated deposits, but it uses rejuvenating herbs, including Fo-ti Tieng, and a variety of hydrocotyle asiatica, believed to rejuvenate the endocrine glands.

A Warning

It is recommended that you do not try this Secret Rite or the Ayuvedic method. Fasting can be dangerous to your health. It can, in fact, result in death. We suggest that you make no changes in your diet without your doctor's permission. We can't stress the point too strongly.

Did Saint Germain Really Exist

There is no question that he did. True, he is said to be a legendary figure, yet records about him were found in the French National Record Office, the French Record Office of Foreign Affairs, the Dutch Palace Archives of Berlin, the Palace and State Archives in Vienna, and the State Archives in Copenhagen.

Startling Facts About St. Germain's Many Lives

The mystery man's first role was that of Francis Bacon, who feigned death in 1624 at the age of 63. Did he really die? Not likely.

He was seen in Venice in 1710. To the French ambassadress, Madame de Gergy, he appeared to be about 45 years old. Yet, when she saw him again in Paris 50 years later, he didn't appear to be a day older. In fact, she thought the man she saw was his son!

The record shows that Saint Germain had been in Venice 23 years earlier, in 1687, and had used the name Signor Gualdi. Oddly enough, when he was questioned about his identity, he left town immediately.

Researchers have traced him to the Polish Rider who, in 1670, delivered discourses to Abbe Monfaucon de Villars which were published under the title, "Comte de Gabalis." The Polish Rider was an actual person, undoubtedly St. Germain, and his picture was painted by Titian. You can see it today in the Frick Collection in New York City. It's probably the only picture extant of Count Saint Germain.

You can also see an autographed letter in his handwriting in the British Museum. It is dated November 22, 1735. A man named Morin, who was the secretary to Baron von Gleichen, said that he had met St. Germain in Holland in 1739.

On December 9, 1745, Horace Walpole stated that the mystery man was in London for two years. This was during the rebellion of Charles Edward, the Young Pretender. Saint Germain came under suspicion, was apprehended, but later released when he was able to prove his innocence. Walpole said, "The other day, they seized an old man who goes by the name of Count Saint Germain. He has been here these two years, and will not tell who he is, or whence, but professes that he does not go by his right name. He sings, plays the violin wonderfully, composes, is mad, and not very sensible...The Prince of Wales has had unsatiated curiosity about him, but in vain.

The famous British writer Bulwer Lytton wrote a novel titled *Zanoni* in which Saint Germain was the central character.

Saint Germain made two trips to India in 1745, and another in the company of Clive and Watson in 1755. He also played an important role in the colonization of America and in the early history of Virginia. Records show that he had a retreat in the Himalayas to which he retired periodically and was a practicing yoga. He was seen assuming yoga postures on certain occasions.'

Was St. Germain A Miracle Man?

Researchers have found evidence that he was a Jacobite in London, a conspirator in St. Petersburg, Russia and an alchemist and connoisseur of paintings in Paris. He was a Russian general in Naples. He was seen fiddling in the music room of Versailles, talking gossip with Horace Walpole in London, reading in Frederick the Great's Library in Berlin, and conducting meetings in the caverns near the Rhine.

E.M. Butler says of him in her book, *Myth of the Magi,* that he had unusual powers. She wrote.

He was also such a brilliant conversationalist, raconteur, so widely traveled, so deeply read, so lighthearted, so urbane, and with all so lavish and so splendid, that he outshone even his own diamonds and sparkling precious stones. Not only did he attain to a prestige, fame and power unparalleled in that cynical, skeptical and sophisticated society, but he maintained that position for a period of three years under the eyes of the great and in the penetrating rays of the fierce light that beats upon a throne. First insinuating himself into the good graces of Madame de Pompadour, he made the conquest of the king by virtue of his inherent power to fascinate, to entertain, to charm, persuade and convince. Louis XV, perennially in the last stages of boredom, and hard indeed to astonish or impress, was nevertheless taken out of himself when this remarkable newcomer transformed one of his flawed diamonds into a stone without blemish, and worth more than three times its original price.

The scintillating star at Court, who was admitted to the petit soupers of the king and to the private apartments of the favorite; the brilliant scientist who was to revolutionize industry and stabilize finance; the wonderful sage who possessed the secret of perpetual rejuvenation and might perhaps impart it to a chosen few, wielded (and indeed it was a foregone conclusion that he would) no negligible influence conclusion that he would) no negligible influence in the political sphere. More than one number of the French cabinet consulted him about affairs of state and even acted upon his advice. Saint Germain was said to be responsible for the fall of the Controller General of Finance, Etienne de Sillhoutte in 1759. He had made himself prominent enough and trusted enough to be charged with overtures of peace with England which were in the air at that time.

The fact that Saint Germain turned a flawed diamond into a perfect stone indicates that he was either a master alchemist or a miracle worker. His perfection in everything he turned his hand to tells us that he must have had an incredible IQ.

The Supreme Alchemist

Count St. Germain had no income, no property, no visible means of support. He did not deal with banks or bankers. For nearly a century he mingled with the royalty of Europe. Although he dressed in simple clothes, he was always arrayed with diamonds and other precious stones. His collection of jewels and precious diamonds was staggering to behold. He had an opal the size of an egg. When he gave a banquet his habit was to place a large precious stone on every place-card. Each was worth thousands of dollars.

How did he do it? The answer had to be through alchemy, that ancient art of chemically changing base metal to gold with other precious metals.

It was believed that Saint Germain was able to change mercury into gold. Admittedly, that can be done today, but it takes a cyclotron, or atom-smashing machine, to do it.

He also possessed the secret of changing low-grade diamonds (today they are called industrial diamonds) into quality stones.

Casanova Distrusted Him

Casanova tells the story of how Saint Germain took a twelve-sol piece and changed it into gold. Casanova told the mystery man that he must have switched one coin for the other. Saint Germain snapped, "Those who are capable of entertaining doubts of my work are not worthy to speak to me." With that, he ushered the famed Italian out of his rooms.

An Eyewitness to the Alchemist's Miracle

The man who actually saw Saint Germain make gold was the Marquis de Valbelle. The Marquis visited the alchemist in his laboratory and found the man busy at his furnaces. Saint Germain asked him for a silver six-franc piece. He then covered it with a black substance and exposed it to the heat of a small flame. The Marquis watched the object change color and become a bright red. Minutes later, the alchemist took the metal out of the cooling vessel and gave it to his friend. It was now pure gold. The coin was held by the Countess d'Adhemar until 1786, when it was stolen.

Occult Chemistry

Saint Germain was quite liberal with his secrets, up to a point. He told friends that he learned his ability at alchemy from a second trip he made to the Far East, and other ancient countries. He said, "I am indebted for my knowledge of melting jewels to my second journey to India.

Another skill he had was the preparation of cosmetics. He introduced new methods of tanning and dyeing, so that he was much in demand by the ladies of the court.

It now becomes easy to understand why he was so popular among the crown heads of Europe. He possessed elixirs to keep one young, he knew the secrets of alchemy, and he knew how to make women look prettier than they really were. But it was his power to change common stones into priceless pieces of jewelry that attracted everyone. Madame de Pompadour said, "This singular man passed for being fabulously rich and he distributed diamonds and jewels with astonishing liberality."

An Astonishing Letter

On October 23, 1778, a man named Dresser wrote to Baron Uffel, judge of the Court of Appeal in Celle:

I must now give your Excellency news of a singular phenomenon. A man calling himself Saint Germain, who refused to make known his origins, is lodging here in the Hotel Kaiserhof. He lives in great style...and yet he never receives any letters of credit. He writes day and night, carries on a correspondence with the greatest crowned heads, but does not care to mix in society, except that of the Countess Bentinck and the French ministers. It is very difficult to get to know him. He is an amateur in the natural sciences, has studied nature; and it is thanks to the knowledge he has received that he is now 182 years of age and looks like a man of forty. In the strictest confidence he told a friend of mine that he possessed certain drops by which he achieves all his results, even the transmutation of metals. In his presence he transformed a copper coin into the finest silver, poor leathers into the best English variety, and semi-precious stones into diamonds. At the same time he is continually alone and by no means expansive. He has a superfluity of all kinds of gold and silver coins, which look as if they had just been minted. And yet he gets no remittances from anyone, nor has he any introductions to the merchants. How does all this come about?

Saint Germain Founded a Modern Industry

The man who performed miracles with gold, silver and precious stones was also a master at the art of dyeing. In 1763 he erected factories in Tournai in which his new process of dyes, colors for painting and leather were applied to silk and other fabrics like wool and wood. At a later date and in cooperation with Prince Charles of Hesse, Saint Germain opened still another factory, thus laying the foundation for an industry that still flourishes.

The Medicine Man

It was a well known fact at the time (the 18th century) that Saint Germain prolonged his own life with the aid of herbal elixir. Oddly, he did not keep this phenomenal medicine to himself, but distributed it to the poor people at will and free of charge. Of course, what he did keep to himself was the recipe for this amazing concoction.

It was also known that the famed intellect, Mesmer, who is credited with the discovery of mesmerism (hypnotism) studied under Saint Germain and derived the theory of animal magnetism from the man of mystery.

A Secret Society

When Francis Bacon, also known as Saint Germain, was in England during the latter part of the 17th century, he founded Rosicrucianism and Freemasonry. Bacon's biographer, a man named Dodd, shows that Shakespeare's plays are full of Masonic symbolism, and it is believed that only a Freemason, not Shakespeare, could have written the plays attributed to the Bard.

Researchers point out that the word "Rosicrucian" comes from the royal emblem of the House of Tudor. Bacon, whose real name was Francis Tudor, the son of Queen Elizabeth, was the last surviving member of the Tudors. The symbol was the rose and the cross.

In an old Mason minute book one can find the signature of Count Saint Germain near that of Marquis de Lafayette. The Founding Fathers of the American Republic were also Freemasons, including Washington and Benjamin Franklin. The latter wore a book on Freemasonry.

What Did He Eat? How Did He Live?

All reports indicate that Saint Germain was a simple man with simple needs. Although he mingled with high society no matter which century he lived in, he was equally happy being alone, and remaining alone for long periods.

We don't know what he ate that helped to keep him alive for so long, but we do know this: Casanova once visited Saint Germain in Belgium and nearly found out the secret diet.

Casanova found his man in confinement. Saint Germain elected to stay cooped up in the house for a great length of time while he experimented with his elixirs and chemicals. Casanova did not immediately get in to see the man. What he saw was some grooms walking a few spirited horses. He asked one of them, "Whose horses are these?"

The groom replied, "To the Count Saint Germain, the adept who has been here a month and never goes out. Everybody who passes through the place wants to see him, but he makes himself visible to no one."

Casanova sent a note in to Saint Germain. The reply was:

The gravity of my occupation compels me to exclude everyone, but in your case I will make an exception. Come whenever you like and you will be shown in. You need not mention my name or your own. I do not ask that you share my repast, for my food is not suitable to others, to you least of all, if your appetite is what it used to be.

Rumor had it at one time that Saint Germain ate nothing; this tale dispels that rumor.

Casanova found the Count with a two-inch beard. After a few opening remarks, Casanova told his host that he suffered from an acute disease. Saint Germain gave him fifteen pills. He said that in three days the disease would be completely gone. And it was.

Casanova did not report on what it was that Saint Germain ate. He saw no dishes on the man's table, no scraps of food anywhere. If the Italian had arrived earlier or later, he might have caught a glimpse of the man's diet.

The Countess De Gergy Meets The Count

One of the earliest accounts written of St. Germain's never-ending escapades can be found in an out-of-print book published in French and quoted by the author, Dr. Raymond Bernard (A.B., M.A., Ph.D.) in his scholarly work, "The Great Secret of Count Saint Germain" (Health Research:

The old countess de Gergy, who fifty years earlier had accompanied her husband to Venice where he had the appointment of ambassador, lately met Saint-Germain at Mme. de Pompadour's. For some time she watched the stranger with signs of the greatest surprise, in which was mixed not a little fear. Finally, unable to control her excitement, she approached the Count more out of curiosity than in fear."

"Will you have the kindness to tell me," said the Countess, "whether your father was in Venice in the year 1710?"

"No, Madame," replied the Count unconcerned, "It is very much longer since I lost my father, but I myself was living at the end of the last and the beginning of this century. I had the honor to pay you court then, and you were kind enough to admire a few Barcaroles of my composing which we used to sing together."

"Forgive me, but that is impossible. The Count Saint-Germain I knew in those days was at least 45 years old; and you, at the outside, are that age at present," the countess replied. "Fifty years ago," she continued, "I was ambassadress at Venice, and I remember seeing you there looking just as you do now, only somewhat riper in age perhaps, for you have grown younger since then."

Bowing low, the Count answered with dignity: "I have always thought myself happy in being able to make myself agreeable to the ladies."

Madame de Gergy continued: "You then have called yourself the Marquis Balletti."

The Count bowed again and replied: "And Countess de Gergy's memory is still as good as it was fifty years ago."

The Countess smiled and said: "That I owe to an elixir you gave me at our first meeting. You are really an extraordinary man."

The Count assumed a grave expression and said: "Did this Marquis Balletti have a bad reputation?"

"On the contrary," replied the Countess, "he was in very good society."

The Count shrugged his shoulders expressively saying, "Well, as no one complains of him, I adopt him willingly as my grandfather."

Since Saint-Germain could not explain to her how he could be the same person and not his own father, he avoided further discussion on the subject by remarking with a smile, "Madame, I am very old."

"But then you must be nearly a hundred years old," added the Countess.

"That is not impossible" was the Count's enigmatical reply.

Countess d'Adhemar was present during the entire conversation and vouches for its accuracy in every detail.

Other evidences of Saint-Germain's great age are afforded by the memoirs of Madame de Hausset, lady-in-waiting to Madame de Pompadour, who wrote down the ensuing conversation that took place between the Madame and the Count, when she took the opportunity to question him about his age, which question, as usual, he cleverly avoided answering. The incident occurred when Saint-Germain was describing historical events of the remote past with a vividness which made even the most incredulous believe that he must have been an eye-witness of what he described. Referring to this fact, Madame de Pompadour laughed and asked, "Apparently, you have seen it all yourself?"

To this the Count replied: "I have a very good memory and I have studied French history in detail. I sometimes amuse myself not by *making* people believe, but by *allowing* them to believe that I have lived in the oldest times.

"Still you never say how old you really are, and you claim to be very old," replied the Madame, adding, "The Countess de Gergy, who was ambassadress fifty years ago, I believe in Venice, declared that she knew you then looking just as you do now."

"It is perfectly true, Madame, that I made the acquaintance of the Countess de Gergy a long time ago," the Count replied.

"But according to her, you must be over a hundred years old now," the Madame said.

"That is not impossible," he replied laughing, "but as I admit, it is even more possible that the revered lady is talking nonsense."

It was through such subterfuges and evasions that he perpetually avoided any definite statement about his age and kept his secret intact, to the consternation and wonderment of his inquirers. It was answers like he gave to Madame de Pompadour that led Gustav Bord to write to Saint-Germain that "he allows a certain mystery to hover about him, a mystery which awakens curiosity and sympathy. Being a virtuoso in the art of misleading, he says nothing that is untrue, but he knows how (by silence rather than by learned discussions) to let people believe the mistaken legends that are current about him. He has the rare gift of remaining silent and profiting by it."

Let us now return to Madame de Hausset's story.

"You gave Madame de Gergy," pressed Madame de Pompadour, "an elixir surprising in its effects. She claims that for a long time she appeared to be no older than twenty-four. Why should you not give some to the king?"

Saint-Germain allowed an expression of feigned terror to spread over his face, said, "Ah, Madame, I should be mad indeed to take it into my head to give the king an unknown drug."

The following is an example of the mischievous and enigmatical manner with which Saint-Germain kept everyone guessing about his age:

"These silly Parisians," he once told Gleichen, "believe that I am 500 years old, and I confirmed them in that belief, for I see that they get a lot of pleasure out of it. Not but what I am immeasurably older than I appear." (From Gleichen's *Souvenirs*, which was first published in 1818.)

As for the far-fetched and exaggerated claims circulating to the fact that Saint-Germain pretended to have been present at the Council of Nicea, and to have conversed with Christ, etc., these originated in an impersonator nicknamed Lord Gower, who introduced himself to Parisian society as Count Saint Germain, and they were not made by the real Saint-Germain, who, because of his unchanging youth down through the centuries, was believed to possess the philosopher's stone and the Elixir of Life, and from this developed puerile anecdotes of old ladies taking too much of the Elixir and becoming little girls, babies or even embryos.

The following conversation is reported between Saint-Germain and Countess de Genlis, then a child of ten:

One evening, at a party, Saint-Germain accompanied several Italian airs for the young Countess, afterwards so celebrated under the name of Countess de Genlis, then aged ten years.

When she finished singing, the Count said to her: "In five or six years, you will have a very beautiful voice, which you will preserve for a long time. In order to perfect its charm you should also preserve your beauty. This will be your happy fate between your 16th and 17th year."

"But, Count," answered the child, while allowing her pretty fingers to glide over the keys, "that does not lie in one's power."

"Oh, yes," answered the Count carelessly, "only tell me whether it would give you pleasure to remain as you are at that age."

"Truly that would be charming," she replied.

"Well, I promise it to you," the Count said, and spoke of other matters.'

We have mentioned that Saint-Germain carried around with him a miniature of a very beautiful woman attached to his arm, who wore a peculiar costume, who he said was his mother. "To what date does that dress belong?" he was asked. Without answering, he put his sleeve down and brought forward another topic. Was she Queen Elizabeth, dressed in the peculiar costume she usually wore?

Saint Germain and the Great Seal of the United States

History reveals the remarkable fact that Saint Germain could very well have assisted the likes of Benjamin Franklin, Thomas Jefferson and John Adams in drafting the Constitution of the United States. First off, we know that the above-named founding fathers of this great land were

Freemasons and members of the Rosicrucian order—the exact same path that Saint Germain followed in his spiritual undertakings. Noting that the Count was not seen in Europe during and directly following the Revolutionary War, it has been suggested that he might have been residing in the countryside near Philadelphia, from where he offered his services to our early leaders.

In my previously published book *Angels of the Lord* (also an INNER LIGHT publication), I dealt with the research of the late Rev. Virginia F. Brasington, and her findings of how the Great Seal of the United States came into being. I revealed how a "mysterious stranger" had approached Thomas Jefferson in his garden late one night after the great statesman had been working all day on behalf of the Continental Congress. Jefferson had been asked to think of a special design for the seal of the newly united thirteen colonies, but found he had a mental block in coming up with anything that would have a significant meaning. Then, out of nowhere, this mysterious figure appeared before his eyes. The man was dressed in a black cloak which had an attached hood that covered his face and said little, except that he had a seal that would be appropriate and meaningful.

Interestingly enough, if you look at the back of the dollar bill you will see that the Great Seal is composed of a representation of a pyramid, its magical thirteen steps leading skyward to a single floating eye. Symbolically, this eye is easily recognized as the "third eye" that enables sensitives and mystics to see into the inner planes—it is also a symbol that Saint Germain would have known about since it was used widely by Rosicrucians and other advanced thinkers in matters involving spirituality.

Think about this for a moment—would Jefferson have agreed to use a symbol on the Great Seal if he hadn't known the true source of the design? Chances are, he knew very well the man in the cape, but could not reveal his identity as Jefferson and the other founding fathers had agreed to keep their interest in metaphysics a secret, since they possessed information which they felt was not ready to be shared with the masses who had not undergone the proper initiation into the mystery schools and secret societies of Europe (branches of which had sprung up in this country under Saint Germain's guidance). You can examine the Great Seal at your own leisure and decide the truth of the matter for yourself.

Saint Germain's Feigned Death

The records show that Saint Germain died on February 27, 1784 on the estate of Prince Charles of Hesse-Cassel in Eckernforde. He contracted rheumatism after living for some time in damp rooms. Records also reveal that he was buried on March 2nd, after being entered in the parish register. Prince Charles considered his passing a great loss. He wrote:

> He was perhaps one of the greatest sages who has ever lived. He loved humanity; he desired money only to give to the poor. He even loved animals, and his heart was occupied with only the happiness of others. He believed he could make mankind happy by procuring for them new pleasures, lovelier cloths and colors; and glorious colors cost almost nothing. I have never known a man with a clearer mind, and at the same time he was possessed of a learning, especially in history, that I have rarely found. He had been in all countries of Europe...but France seemed to be the land which he lived best.

That was certainly a fine eulogy, but was Saint Germain really dead?

Doubts Persist

There was a mock funeral for Francis Bacon in 1624; he showed up later in Germany. Apparently the same thing happened in the late 1700s, after Saint Germain died in 1784.

Noted occult figure Manly Hall wrote:

> The strange circumstances connected with the passing lead us to suspect that it was a mock funeral similar to that given the English adept, Lord Bacon.
>
> Great uncertainty and vagueness surround his latter days, for no confidence can be reposed in the announcement of the death of one illuminate by another, for, as is well known, all means to secure the end were in their code justifiable and it may have been to the interests of the society that Saint Germain should have been thought dead.

Famed seer Madame Blavatsky said:

Is it not absurd to suppose that if he really died at the time and place mentioned, he would have been laid in the ground without the pomp and ceremony, the official supervision, the police registration, which attend the funerals of men of his rank and notoriety? Where are these data? He passed out of public sight more than a century ago (Madame Blavatsky founded Theosophy in the 1800s), and positive proof that he was living several years after 1784. He is said to have had a most important private conference with the Empress of Russia in 1785 or 1786 and to have appeared to the Princess of Lambelle when she stood before the Tribunal, a few moments before she was struck down with a bullet, and a butcher-boy cut off her head; and to Jeanne Dubarry, the mistress of Louis XV, as she waited on her scaffold at Paris for the stroke of the guillotine in the Days of Terror of 1793.

Further Proof

He had been seen in many places and by many people since his supposed death in 1784. Distinguished historians have noted that Saint Germain was seen in the 19th century and in the early part of the 20th century. He was seen at a Masonic convention in Paris in 1785, one year after his alleged death. In 1788, Count de Chalons told the Countess d'Adhemar that when he returned from the Embassy in Venice he talked with Saint Germain in the Plaza of St. Mark on the night of his departure as ambassador to Portugal.

An Amazing Account

The Countess d'Adhemar wrote in her memoirs that she had seen Saint Germain six times since the year of his "death." She saw him first in 1785 in Paris, at a chapel of the Franciscans. That meeting occurred after he wrote to her warning her of the dangers that awaited the royal couple. At the end of a long conversation, she said, to him, "When will I see you again?"

"Five more times," he replied.

The prediction was fulfilled. A year before she died, the Countess wrote in a note dated May 12, 1821: "I have seen Saint Germain, and to my greatest amazement at the death of the Queen (October 6, 1793), at the coming of the 18th Brumaire (November 9, 1799), on the morning of the death of Duc d'Enghien (March 15, 1804), in the month of January 1815, and on the eve of the murder of the Duc de Berri (1820)."

Saint Germain Still Lives!

The great adept apparently spent most of the 19th century in Tibet, undoubtedly learning as much as possible about the art of longevity. Since he had already lived for four centuries at that time, it was likely that his role in Tibet was as a teacher rather than as a student. Tibetans have a reputation as long livers, but it is doubtful that any of them matched the record set by Saint Germain.

He emerged again in the 20th century. A writer named Leadbeater wrote in his book, *The Masters of the Path*, that he had met Saint Germain in Rome in 1925:

The other adept whom I had the privilege of encountering physically was the Master, the Comte de St. Germain, called sometimes Prince Rakoczy. I met him under quite ordinary circumstances (without any previous appointment, and, as though by chance) walking down the Corso in Rome, dressed as any Italian gentleman. He took me up into the gardens of the Pincian Hill, and we sat for more than an hour talking about the Theosophical Society and its work.

Saint Germain was also seen by other people during that period. In 1932 the head of a Masonic society in Costa Rica reported that he had received a letter from him which came from the Carpathian Mountains. Barbara Moore-Pataleewa, a Russian doctor, who specialized in rejuvenation in England, said she once met him personally. Ninon de l'Enclos learned the secret of rejuvenation from Saint Germain and looked like a young woman even at the age of 90.

Where is Saint Germain Now?

One theory is that he is a member of the "Great White Lodge" of Ascended Masters who make their worldly headquarters in the Himalayas.

The second theory is that he has entered a subterranean world to escape the many impurities that are infecting our atmosphere. Here he can live in peace and no longer have to travel under assumed names.

The Brazilian Theosophical Society, which has a large temple dedicated to "Agharta" (the Subterranean World) at San Lourenzo, Minas Gerais, Brazil, says that Saint Germain is living in the subterranean world with other great Masters.

Charles A. Marcoux, of Subsurface Research Center in Phoenix, Arizona, has been searching for the entrance to that underworld for 20 years. He says: "I want to comment concerning one thing that may be of interest, pertaining to Count Saint Germain. Such a party has contacted me on several occasions, at least he claimed to be Saint Germain."

A Famous Beauty Profited From Saint Germain's Counsel

We said earlier that Ninon de l'Enclos learned the secret of rejuvenation from the Master. Because of his advice she became one of the most beautiful women of France. Everyone was in awe not only of her good looks but because she was able to stay young-looking into advanced age. When she was eighty, one of her grandsons was so charmed by her beauty that he fell in love with her. When that love was not returned, he became so distraught that he committed suicide.

Ninon was forever being questioned about her secret to long life and beauty. As far as anyone knows, she did not go into any details about how Saint Germain helped her to stay young, but she did reveal to the curious that she bathed several times a day in pure water.

Alchemists leave the impression that they have total control over the environment.

The Count has always lived in grand style. For example, he befriended Louis XV who gave him a residence in the Royal Castle of Chambord.

The Ancient Art
of Alchemy

Since the Count was reputed to be a master of the art of alchemy, we should provide a basis for such a belief, and a brief background of the history of this mystical science.

There is the lingering notion among present-day alchemists that physical things have a spiritual parallel. The idea stems from the originator of alchemy, who was believed to have been the Greek god Hermes. He allegedly saw the link between our world and the divine when he guided the souls of the dead to the underworld.

Achieving material transmutation always went hand in hand with attempts to reach spiritual perfection. The alchemist's dream was to attain a god-like state. The thought was that if he could do that, then he might have the power of transformation, such as the power Christ had when he transformed water into wine. The dream, of course, was for the majority who tried unattainable, and there were those who searched greedily for an easy way to make gold from metal But two present-day authors remind us that after studying alchemical books and manuscripts they concluded that alchemy is the only parareligious activity that has contributed to our knowledge of science.

The authors are Louis Pauwels and Jacques Bergier, who said in their book, *The Dawn of Magic:*

"We have heard a learned scientist affirm that since repetitions of the process of refining and purifying metals and metalloids do not in any way alter their properties, the recommendations of the alchemists in this connection could be considered as a kind of mystic lesson in patience, a ritual gesture, like telling the beads of a rosary. And yet it is just by such a refing process and the technique described by the alchemists, known today as 'zone fushion,' that the germanium and silicon used in transistors is prepared. We know now...that by purifying a metal very thoroughly and then introducing minute quantities, some millionths of a gram, of impurities…the substance treated is endowed with new and revolutionary properties."

Some alchemists are considered today to be pioneers in science: These men were obviously less interested in changing metal to gold than in searching for benefits for mankind.

Albertus Magnus (1193–1280): He was the first to describe the chemical composition of cinnabar, whitelead, and minium.

Paracelsus (1493–1541): He introduced the medical use of chemical compounds.

Johann-Baptiste della Porta (1538–1615): He recognized the existence of gases.

These were scores of others too numerous to mention here, but all of them believed that during their scientific experiments there sometimes occurred a spiritual transmutation. Any change that occurred in the alchemist's laboratory also occurred in his soul.

Pauwels and Bergier wrote: "All the traditional texts stress this phenomenon and evoke the moment when the 'Great Work' is accomplished and the alchemist becomes an 'awakened man.' It would seem that these old texts describe in this way the final stage of all real knowledge of the laws of matter and of energy, including technical knowledge."

Paracelsus, Healer

The Swiss alchemist and healer, born in 1493, was a learned physician whose fame spread because of his great abilities to heal the sick. He did have a knowledge of alchemy, which led him to search out the possibility of extracting medicine from mineral substances. In his day, herbal remedies were traditional. This alchemist is credited with performing cures that bordered on the miraculous, yet he refused to take credit for them, saying that the health of the body cannot be achieved without the well-being of the soul that dwells within it.

Count Cagliostro, Charlatan?

He was born Guiseppe Balsamo in Palermo, Sicily in 1743. The figure he presented to the world was flamboyant and mysterious. Cagliostro claimed that he was the master of every branch of magic, including alchemy. His greatest exploit in alchemy, if true, was the manufacture of a huge and brilliant diamond, which he offered to the French Cardinal Louis de Rohan.

Another amazing feat, which would certainly be welcomed in day's world, was his ability to forecast the winning numbers in lotteries. He did that in London, convincing large numbers of people of his magical powers when he correctly announced the winning lottery numbers several times in a row.

Cagliostro was famous throughout Europe, though he made the mistake of practicing what was deemed to be witchcraft in several countries. For those offenses he spent quite a lot of time in various jails. Nevertheless, upon his release from the Bastille in 1786, he was greeted by a throng of 10,000 who turned out to acclaim him.

Roger Bacon, Alchemist and Amazing Prophet

Bacon was the first Englishman to embrace the philosophy of alchemy. He was born in Somerset in 1214 and was considered a genius before he reached his majority. Astronomers were extremely rare at that time, so Bacon became one, and we are indebted to him for rectifying the Julian Calendar, with regard to the solar year. In 1267 he presented his findings to Pope Clement IV, but the work was not put into practice until Gregory became pope, hence the Gregorian Calendar.

Bacon was obsessed with the properties of lenses and convex glasses. He invented spectacles and achromatic lenses, the theory, and possibly the first construction of the telescope.

His own letters reveal that he was a unique prophet, saying in one of them that some day there would be machines constructed for navigation that would dispense with the need for rowers, and that the vessels would glide through the water at tremendous speeds.

In another letter he states: "It is equally possible to construct cars which may be set in motion with marvelous rapidity, independently of horses or other animals. Flying machines may also be made, the man seated in the center, and by means of certain contrivances beating the air with artificial wings."

Bacon also envisioned the crane, diving equipment, suspension bridges, adding that all of these things were known to the ancients and would eventually be rediscovered.

One Bacon biographer said, "Should we be surprised if all of these prodigies obtained for him the name of magician in an age of superstition and ignorance? The friars of his own order refused to let his works into their library, as if he were a man who ought to be proscribed by society. His persecution increased till, in 1278, he was imprisoned and forced to confess his repentance of his pains in the arts and sciences. He was constrained to abandon the house of his order, and to form a retreat where he might work in peace."

Bacon's reputation as a magician spread over Western Europe, but with it there persisted a rumor that his wisdom came from demons.

Despite censure, Bacon continued his work in alchemy. He studied the properties of saltpeter, and although he may not have discovered gunpowder, he contributed to its perfection by teaching the purification of saltpeter by its dissolution in water and by crystallization. He also noted the chemical role played by the air in combustion.

Is Transmutation Possible?

The celebrated Italian philosopher Claude Berigard wrote about his own experience with transmutation in his book, *Circulus Pisanus,* published in 1641.

"I did not think that it was possible to convert quicksilver into gold, but an acquaintance thought proper to remove my doubt. He gave me about a drachm of a powder nearly the color of wild poppy, and having a smell like calcined sea-salt. To avoid all imposition, I purchased a crucible, charcoal, and quicksilver, in which I was certain that there was no gold mixed. Ten drachms of quicksilver which I heated on the fire were on projection transmuted into nearly the same weight of good gold, which stood all tests. Had I not performed this operation in the most careful manner, taking every precaution against the possibility of doubt, I should not have believed it, but I am satisfied of the fact."

The Greedy Search for Gold

Kings and governments were caught up in the search for ways to turn metal into gold and thereby enrich themselves and their countries. But it wasn't easy to find true alchemists willing to do their bidding.

The Senate of Venice hired a Cypriot alchemist in the late 16th century to brace up the republic's crumbling finances. The effort was not successful.

Charles II of England built an alchemical laboratory under his bedchamber. He worked diligently to produce gold, heedless of the violent explosions he caused, but did not succeed.

James IV of Scotland hired an alchemist who failed to make gold. He also failed in his attempt to fly. He attached a pair of feathered wings to his body and leaped from the battlements of Stirling Castle. He fell like a rock and broke his leg.

Christian IV of Denmark in the 1640s may have had better luck. He had coins made from alchemical gold. Several other monarchs had similar coins and medals struck. In 1675, while Emperor Leopold watched, an alchemist converted copper and tin into gold. Two years later he same alchemist turned a silver medallion into gold. The medallion was examined in 1888 and found to have a specific gravity between gold and silver.

The goal of all alchemists was to make Stone, which had the power to turn all things into gold. J.B. van Helmont, a 17th century chemist and the inventor of the term "gas," described the stone in his *DeVita Eterna*:

"I have seen and handled more than once the Stone of the Philosophers: in color it was like powder of saffron but heavy and shining, even as powdered glass. There was given to me on a certain occasion the fourth part of the grain, or the six-hundredths of an ounce. Having wrapped it in paper, I made projection therewith upon the eight ounces of quicksilver, heated in a crucible, and immediately all the quicksilver—having made a little noise—was congealed into a yellow mass. This being melted in a strong fire, I found eight ounces minus eleven grains of most pure gold."

A member of numerous brotherhoods, St. Germain held the highest of positions in the Freemasons, going from lodge to lodge as a master adept.

St. Germain—
"Obermohr" of
Many Mystic Brotherhoods

It should not surprise anyone to find out that St. Germain has been highly regarded in mystical circles during his lengthy lifetime.

A debate has raged for literally centuries as to what Secret Societies he might have actually belonged to. There are some who claim he was active as a Freemason in France, while others maintain that he followed the teachings of the Rosicrucians. Actually there is evidence that at certain times in his life he has been very influential in various metaphysical groups in order to aid in the cause of humankind's spiritual evolution.

In 1908 popular occult writer A. Mailly penned the following paragraphs that back up our thesis that St. Germain was a true adept who saw it within his wisdom to spread words of enlightenment under various banners.

In the Masonic and Rosicrucian literature one often finds hints as to the relations of St. Germain to the secret societies of Austria. One of St. Germain's adherents in Vienna was Count J. F. von Kufstein, in whose Lodge (in the house of Prince Auersberg) magical meetings were held which generally lasted from 11 p.m. to 6 a.m. St. Germain was present at one such meeting and expressed his satisfaction with the workings.

...St. Germain collected old pictures and portraits; he was addicted to alchemy, believed in universal medicine and made studies as to animal magnetism. He impressed people, especially the higher classes, by his French manners, his wide knowledge and his talkativeness. This "Bohemian" so much attracted by historians, played the part of a political agent during the peace negotiations between France and Austria. Again, he is said to have distinguished himself in the year 1792 in the revolution.

He was the "Obermohr" of many mystic brotherhoods, where he was worshipped as a superior being and where every one believed in his "sudden" appearances and equally "sudden" disappearances. He belongs to the picture of "Old Vienna" with its social mysteriousness; where it was swarming with Rosicrucians, Asiatics, Illuminates, Alchemists, Magnetopaths, Thaumaturgs, Templars, who all of them had many and willing adherents.

Dr. Mesmer who knew the Comte St. Germain well from his stay in Paris, requested him to come to Vienna in order that he might pursue his study of animal magnetism with him. St. Germain stayed secretly here and was then known as the "American of the Felderhof" which latter became later on "Laszia House" in the Lugeck N. 3. Dr. Mesmer was much helped by the Count and here in Vienna his (Mesmer's) teaching was written down. Soon Mesmer gained followers but he was obliged to leave the town. He went to Paris where his "Harmonious Society"—a secret society of savants—continued to exist. In Vienna St. Germain came in touch with many mystagogues. He visited the famous laboratory of the Rosicrucians in the Landstrasse behind the hospital where he instructed for some time his brethren in the sciences of Solomon. The Landstrasse, situated on the outskirts of Vienna, was for many centuries a region of spooks.

Below in the Erdberg the Templars and the estates of their order and outside town in the Simmering there was in the times of Rudolf II, the gold kitchen where the eccentric fraternity endeavoured to make gold. It is certain that the Comte de St. Germain has been in Vienna in the year 1735, and also later. The arrival of the Count (who enjoyed at that time a great prestige) at once created a great sensation in the initiated circles.

Today, a number of metaphysical or New Age organizations herald St. Germain as a favorite messenger, often claiming to receive channeled messages from the master teacher who is said to be in seclusion in Tibet, residing in an underground city, as part of the "Great White Brotherhood" (an order that is responsible for beaming telepathic messages to students all over the world). Later in this book we will present special examples of such channeling received through William Alexander Oribello.

As yet another example, the Theosophical Society has long cherished St. Germain as one of their own and have almost single-handedly kept his name alive in their literature. Their extensive work, *The Comte De St. Germain—The Secret of Kings* written by Isabel Cooper-Oakley in 1911 is perhaps the most valuable biographical reference obtainable on this important man, who maintains his supreme position in the era which has commonly become known as the New Age of Enlightenment.

Though there have been those who have come forward to say that St. Germain was regarded only as a charlatan by leading Masons, Cooper-Oakley's extensive investigation has proven this claim untrue. Her findings as outlined in the following pages are quite conclusive in this regard!

In modern Freemason literature the effort is made to eliminate his name, and even, in some instances, to assert that he had no real part in the Masonic movement of the last century and was regarded only as a charlatan by leading Masons. Careful research, however, into the Masonic archives proves this to be untrue; indeed, the exact contrary can be shown, for M. de St. Germain was one of the selected representatives of the French Masons at their great convention in Paris in 1785. As one account says: "The Germans who distinguished themselves on this occasion were Bade, von Dalberg, Forster, Duke Ferdinand of Brunswick, Baron de Gleichen, Russworm, von Wöllner, Lavater, Ludwig Prince of Hesse, Ross-Kampf, Stork, Thaden von Wächter....The French were honourably represented by *St. Germain,* St. Martin, Touzet-Duchanteau, Etteila, Mesmer, Dutrousset, d'Hérecourt, and Cagliostro."

The same category of names, but with more detail, is given by N. Deschamps. We find Deschamps speaking of M. de St. Germain as one of the Templars. An account is also given of the initiation of Cagliostro by the Comte de St. Germain, and the ritual used on this occasion is said to have been that of the knights Templar. It was in this year also that a group of Jesuits brought the wildest and most disgraceful accusations against M. de St. Germain, M. de St. Martin and many others, accusations of immorality, infidelity, anarchy, etc. The charges were levelled at the Philaletheans, or "Rite des Philalètes ou Chercheurs de la Vérité," founded 1773 in the Masonic Lodge of "Les Amis-Réunis." Prince Karl of Hesse, Savalette de Tavanne, Count de Gebelin, and all the really mystic students of the time were in this Order. The Abbé Barruel indicted the whole body, individually and collectively, in terms so violent and on charges so unfounded that even non-Masons and anti-Mystics protested. He accused M. de St. Germain and his followers of being Jacobins, of fomenting and inciting the Revolution, of atheism and immorality.

These charges were carefully investigated and rejected as worthless by J.J. Mounier, a writer who was neither Mystic nor Mason, but only a lover of honest dealing. Mounier says: "There are accusations so atrocious, that before adopting them a just man must seek the most authentic testimony; he who fears not to publish them, without being in the position to give decided proofs, should be severely punished by law and, where the law fails, by all right-minded people. Such is the procedure adopted by M. Barruel against a Society that used to meet at Ermenonville after the death of Jean Jacques Rousseau, under the direction of the Charlatan St. Germain."

This view appears to be well corroborated, and is upheld by various writers;. in fact, the proof is conclusive that M. de St. Germain had nothing to do with the Jacobin party as the Abbé Barruel and the Abbé Migne have tried to insist.

Another writer says: "At this time Catholic Lodges were formed in Paris; their protectors were the Marquises de Girardin and de Bouillé. Several Lodges were held at Ermenonville, the property of the first-named. Their chief aim was "d'établir une communication entre Dieu et l'homme par le moyen des êtres intermédiaires.' "

Now both the Marquis de Giradin and the Marquis de Bouillé were staunch Royalists and Catholics; it was the latter, moreover, who aided the unhappy Louis XVI. and his family in their attempted escape. Again, both of these Catholic nobles were personal friends of M. de St. Germain; hence it hardly appears possible that the assertions of the Abbés Barruel and Migne had any veracious foundation, since the establishing of "Catholic Lodges" certainly does not appear atheistical in tendency, nor the close friendship of true Royalists alarmingly revolutionary. According to the well-known writer Éliphas Lévi, M. de St. Germain was a Catholic in outward religious observance. Although he was the founder of the Order of St. Joachim in Bohemia, he separated himself from this society as soon as revolutionary theories began to spread among its members.

Some of the assemblies in which the Comte de St. Germain taught his philosophy were held in the Rue Platrière; other meetings of the "Philalètes" were held in the Lodge "des Amis-Réunis" in the Rue de la Sourdiere.

According to some writers, there was a strong Rosicrucian foundation—from the true Rosicrucian tradition—in this Lodge. It appears that the members were studying the conditions of life on higher planes, just as Theosophists of today are doing. Practical occultism and spiritual mysticism were the end and aim of the Phila-letheans; but alas, the karma of France overwhelmed them, and scenes of bloodshed and violence swept them and their peaceful studies away.

A fact that disturbed the enemies of the Comte de St. Germain was the personal devotion of his friends, and that these friends treasured his portrait. In the d'Urfé collection, in 1783, was a picture of the mystic engraved on copper, with the inscription:—

"The Comte de St. Germain, celebrated Alchemist," followed by the words:

"Ainsi que Prométhée, il déroba la feu,

    Par qui le monde existe et par qui tout respire;

La nature à sa voix obéit et se meurt.

    S'il n'est pas Dieu lui-mˆeme, un Dieu puissant l'inspire."

This copper-plate engraving was dedicated to the Comte de Milly, an intimate friend of M. de St. Germain, a well-known man of the period, and Chevalier de l'Ordre Royal et Militaire de St. Louis, et de l'Aigle Rouge de Braunschweig. This unlucky portrait, however, produced a furious attack from Dr. Biester, the editor of the *Berlinische Monatschrift,* in June 1785. Amongst some amusing diatribes, the following is worthy of notice, if only to show how inaccurate an angry editor can be. As we have already seen, M. de St. Germain was in the year 1785 chosen representative at the Masonic Conference in Paris. Nevertheless, Herr Dr. Biester, in the *same* year, opens his remarks with the astonishing statement: "This adventurer, who died *two years ago* in Danish Holstein"!

Our editor then proceeds to clinch the argument as follows: "I even know that tho' he is dead, many now believe that he is still living, and will soon come forth alive! Whereas he is dead as a door-nail, probably mouldering and rotting as any ordinary man who cannot work miracles, and whom no price has ever greeted."

Ignorance alone must excuse our editor from the charge of being a literary Ananias; but indeed in our own days critics of matters occult are just as ignorant and equally positive as they were a century ago, no matter what their learning in other respects.

And indeed there was some justification for the statements of Herr Dr. Biester, for a more recent writer says:—

"The church register of Eckernförde shows St. Germain died on February 27th, 1784 in this town in whose church he was entombed quite privately on March 2nd. In the church register we read as follows; "Deceased on February 27th, buried on March 2nd, 1784 the so-called Comte de St. Germain and Weldon—further information not known—privately deposited in this church." In the church accounts it is said: "On March 1st, for the here deceased Comte de St. Germain a tomb in the Nicolai Church here in the burial-place sub N. I, 30 years time of decay 10 Rthlr. and for opening of the same 2 Rthlr., in all 12 Rthlr." Tradition tells that the landgrave afterwards got St. Germain buried in Slesvig in the Friederiksberg churchyard there in order to consult his ghost in late hours of the night. On the third of April the mayor and the council of Eckernförde gave legal notice concerning his estate. In that it is said: "As the Comte de St. Germain, known abroad, as also here, under the name of Comte de St. Germain and Weldon, who during the last four years has been living in this country, died recently here in Eckernförde, his effects have been legally sealed, and it has been found necessary as well to his eventual intestate heirs, as until now nothing has been ascertained concerning a left will…etc.…Therefore all creditors are called upon to come forward with their claims on October 14th."

This passage shows definitely that M. de St. Germain was well known under the name of Welldown (it is written in very many different ways).

But—as to the death—we have much evidence that he did not die: Madame d'Adhémar says speaking of M. de St. Germain:—

"He is believed to have deceased in 1784, at Schleswig, when with the Elector of Hesse-Cassel; the Count de Châlons, however, on returning from his Venetian embassy in *1788,* told me of his having spoken to the Comte de Saint-Germain in the Place Saint Marc the day before he left Venice to go on an embassy to Portugal. I saw him again on one other occasion."

And *again from a Masonic* source we get the following statement:—

"Amongst the Freemasons invited to the great conference at Wilhelmsbad 15th Feb. 1785 we find St. Germain included with St. Martin and many others."

And again from a thoroughly Catholic source: the late Librarian of the Great Ambrosiana Library at Milan says:—

"And when, in order to bring about a conciliation between the various sects of the Rosicrucians, the Necromantists, the Cabalist,s the Illuminati, the Humanitarians, there was held a great Congress at Wilhelmsbad, then in the Lodge of the 'Amici riuniti' there also was Cagliostro, with St. Martin, Mesmer and Saint-Germain."

Evidence there is on both sides, and "Church records" are not always infallible; how many a *cause célèbre* has arisen from a fictitious death. If the Comte de St. Germain wished to disappear from public life, this was the best way to accomplish his wish.

His Travels to Meet Mesmer

Mesmer was the forerunner of modern hypnosis, thus the term mesmerize when placing someone into a trance-induced state. His involvement with what was then known as magnetism was the rage of all of Europe, as just about every party or social function of the day had to include a demonstration of Mesmer's seemingly supernatural powers in order to be an acknowledged success. Mesmer, himself, lived in Austria and it is said that St. Germain journeyed around 1889 or 1890 to meet this renowned man.

Franz Gräffer, a Rosicrucian and close friend of St. Germain's, has left us this startling account of the Count's travels to this country

"An unknown man had come on a short visit to Vienna.

"But his sojourn there extended itself.

"His affairs had reference to a far-off time, namely, the twentieth century.

"He had really come to Vienna to see one person only.

"This person was Mesmer, still a very young man.

"Mesmer was struck by the appearance of the stranger. 'You must be the man,' said he, 'whose anonymous letter I received yesterday from the Hague?'

'I am he.'

" 'You wish to speak with me today, at this hour, on my ideas concerning magnetism?'

" 'I wish to do so.'

" 'It was the man who has just left me, who in a fatherly way has guided my ideas in this channel. He is the celebrated astronomer Hell.'

" 'I know it.'

" 'My fundamental ideas, however, are still chaotic; who can give me light?'

" 'I can do so.'

" 'You would make me happy, sir.'

" 'I have to do so.'

"The stranger motioned Mesmer to lock the door.

"They sat down.

"The kernel of their conversation centrered round the theory of obtaining the elements of the elixir of life by the employment of magnetism in a series of permutations.

"The conference lasted three hours....

"They arranged a further meeting in Paris. Then they parted."

That St. Germain and Mesmer were connected in the mystical work of the last century we know from other sources, and that they again met and worked together in Paris, is verified by research among the records of the Lodge meetings already mentioned. This meeting in Vienna must have taken place before Mesmer began his work in Paris judging by the context. Vienna was the great centre for the Rosicrucians and other allied Societies, such as the "Asiatische Brüder," the "Ritter des Lichts," etc. The former were the largest body who really occupied themselves deeply with alchemical researches and had their laboratory in the Landstrasse, behind the Hospital. Among them we find a group of St. Germain's followers.

To quote Franz Gräffer again:—

"One day the report was spread that the Comte de St. Germain, the most enigmatical of all incomprehensibles, was in Vienna. An electric shock passed through all who knew his name. Our Adept circle was thrilled through and through: St. Germain was in Vienna!...

"Barely had Gräffer [his brother Rudolph] recovered from the surprising news, than he flies to Hiniberg, his country seat, where he has his papers. Among these is to be found a letter of recommendation from Casanova, the genial adventurer whom he got to know in Amsterdam, addressed to St. Germain.

"He hurries back to his house of business; there he is informed by the clerk: 'An hour or so a gentleman has been here whose appearance has astonished us all. This gentleman was neither tall nor short, his build was strikingly proportionate, everything about him had the stamp of nobility....He said in French, as it were to himself, not troubling about anyone's presence, the words: "I live in Fedalhofe, the room in which Leibnitz lodged in 1713." We were about to speak, when he was already gone. This last hour we have been, as you see, sir, petrified.'...

"In five minutes Fedalhofe is reached. Liebnitz's room is empty. Nobody knows when 'the American gentleman' will return home. As to luggage, nothing is to be seen but a small iron chest. It is almost dinner time. But who would think of dining! Gräffer is mechanically urged to go and find Baron Linden; he finds him at the 'Ente.' They drive to the Landstrasse, whither a certain something, an obscure presentiment, impels them to drive post haste.

"The laboratory is unlocked; a simultaneous cry of astonishment escapes both; at a table is seated St. Germain, calmly reading a folio, which is a work of Paracelsus. They stand dumb at the threshold; the mysterious intruder slowly closes the book, and slowly rises. Well know the two perplexed men that this apparition can be no other in the world than the man of wonders. The description of the clerk was as a shadow against a reality. It was as if a bright splendour enveloped his whole form. Dignity and sovereignty declared themselves. The men were speechless. The Count steps forward to meet them; they enter. In measured tones, without formality, but in an indescribably ringing tenor, charming the innermost soul, he says in French to Gräffer: 'You have a letter of introduction from Herr von Seingalt; but it is not needed. This gentlemen is Baron Linden. I knew that you would both be here at this moment. You have another letter for me from Brühl. But the painter is not to be saved; his lung is gone, he will die July 8th, 1805. A man who is still a child called Buonaparte will be indirectly to blame. And now, gentlemen, I know of your doings; can I be of any service to you? Speak.' But speech was not possible.

"Linden laid a small table, took confectionery from a cupboard in the wall, placed it before him and went into the cellar.

"The Count signs to Gräffer to sit down, seats himself and says: 'I knew your friend Linden would retire, he was compelled. I will serve you alone. I know you through Angelo Soliman, to whom I was able to render service in Africa. If Linden comes I will send him away again,' Gräffer recovered himself; he was, however, too overwhelmed to respond more than with the words: 'I understand you: I have a presentiment.'

"Meanwhile Linden returns and places two bottles on the table. St. Germain smiles thereat with an indescribable dignity. Linden offers him refreshment. The Count's smile increases to a laugh. 'I ask you,' said he, ' is there any soul on this earth who has ever seen me eat or drink?' He points to the bottles and remarks: 'This Tokay is not direct from Hungary. It comes from my friend Katherine of Russia. She was so well pleased with the sick man's paintings of the engagement at Mödling, that she sent a cask of the same.' Gräffer and Linden were astounded; the wine had been bought from Casanova.

"The Count asked for writing materials; Linden brought them. The 'Wundermann' cuts from a sheet of paper two quarters of the sheet, places them quite close to each other, and seizes a pen with either hand simultaneously. He writes with both, half a page, signs alike, and says: 'You collect autographs, sir; choose one of these sheets, it is a matter of indifference which; the content is the same.' 'No, it is magic,' exclaim both friends, 'stroke for stroke, both handwritings agree, no trace of difference, unheard of!'

"The writer smiles; places both sheets on one another; holds them up against the window-pane; it seems as if there were only one writing to be seen, so exactly is one the facsimile of the other; they appear as if they were impressions from the same copper-plate. The witnesses were struck dumb.

"The Count then said: 'One of these sheets I wish delivered to Angelo as quick as possible. In a quarter of an hour he is going out with Prince Lichtenstein; the bearer will receive a little box....'

"St. Germain then gradually passed into a solemn mood. For a few seconds he became rigid as a statue, his eyes, which were always expressive beyond words, became dull and colourless. Presently, however, his whole being became reanimated. He made a movement with his hand as if in signal of his departure, then said: 'I am leaving (*ich scheide*); do not visit me. Once again will you see me. Tomorrow night I am off; I am much needed in Constantinople; then in England, there to prepare two inventions which you will have in the next century—trains and steamboats. These will be needed in Germany. The seasons will gradually change—first the spring, then the summer. It is the gradual cessation of time itself, as the announcement of the end of the cycle. I see it all; astrologers and meteorologists know nothing, believe me; one needs to have studied in the Pyramids as I have studied. Towards the end of this century I shall disappear out of Europe, and betake myself to the region of the Himalayas. I will rest; I must rest. Exactly in eighty-five years will people again set eyes upon me. Farewell, I love you.' After these solemnly uttered words, the Count repeated the sign with his hand. The two adepts, overpowered by the force of such unprecedented impressions, left the room in a condition of complete stupefaction. In the same moment there fell a sudden heavy shower, accompanied by a peal of thunder. Instinctively they return to the laboratory for shelter. They open the door. St. Germain is no more there....

"Here, my story ends. It is from memory throughout. A peculiar irresistible feeling has compelled me to set down these transactions in writing once more, after so long a time, just today, June 15th, 1843.

"Further, I make this remark, that these events have not been hitherto reported. So herewith do I take my leave."

Though we may possibly never know all the secrets of St. Germain's life, his philosophy or his many discoveries, a lot definitely can be learned through meditation techniques and by contemplation of of the body of literature available on his lifelong works. We believe the book you are now reading is a serious contribution toward preserving and presenting his words and message to modern day seekers of esoteric wisdom and knowledge.

Timothy Green Beckley in front of the late George Van Tassell's "Rejuvenation Machine" which stands on the desert in Yucca Valley, Calif. where it waits to be completed. (Photo by Gabriel Green)

Can Anyone
Live Forever?

Saint Germain apparently has, but only through his mysterious elixirs. There are those who feel that life can be eternal if one feels like living forever. Emerson said: "Immortality will come to such as are fit for it."

What he meant by that is that when one's mind and spirit are buoyant, and when one is in good health without feeling pain or depression, one feels as though life can go on indefinitely. It is only when we hurt, and when we have sorrow, that the notion of eternal life is repugnant.

Physical Immortality Is Possible

Scientists have affirmed in recent years that the body can live for an incredibly long time if the individual refuses to abuse it. The fact is that you can be immortal. William A. Hammond, a New York medical scientist and a former surgeon-general of the United States Army, says: "There is no physiological reason at the present day why man should die."

W.R.C. Latson, a well-known medical scientist in New York and editor of a magazine called *Health Culture*, says:

Mr. Gaze advances the somewhat startling claim that somatic death, that is, the death of the body as a whole, is due to causes which may be averted; and that, by proper means, one may so control the bodily functions as to retain the body indefinitely. I do not hesitate to say that, while his conception of life and the possibility of physical immorality is unique, there is nothing in the accepted facts of physiological science, by which his position can be refuted.

Three Startling Facts About The Body

1. The body is changing constantly. When it does not change, that is

when we grow old. The body completely returns to dust in less than one year. During that period, a new body is constructed, molecule by molecule.

2. The secret of immortal youth—and the secret which Saint Germain undoubtedly knew—is that a conscious cooperation with body changes will prevent old age from creeping up.

3. You can prevent old age and somatic death by being aware of the conditions which bring about both. It is possible to control the vital energies that are sapped by advancing years.

Age—Mind Over Matter

The *London Lancet* reported not long ago about an English girl who was disappointed in love. She was under twenty. She then became insane and lost all track of time. Her belief was that she was living in the same hour that her lover went away. She stood daily at her window to await his return, and took no note of the passing years. Because she was unaware of time, she did not grow older. She was 74 years old when she was noticed by some travelers. She had no wrinkles and no gray hair. The observers guessed that she was a young woman. They saw only youth on her cheeks and brow. How old did they guess she was? Under twenty!

You have probably read about cases in which people who have passed the three score ten years allotted to us are suddenly taking on youthful appearances. Some grow new hair. Some cut new teeth. If you were to talk to these people you would undoubtedly learn that they have learned how to cooperate with their bodily changes, that their outlook on life is rosy, that they are in good health and work hard to maintain that good health.

Do We Need to Eat to Live?

It was mentioned earlier that Saint Germain's diet differed so greatly from the normal fare that he would not invite Casanova to dine with him because his menu was not suitable to the great Italian.

The story may or may not be true. There are those who feel that Saint Germain never ate at all. Far-fetched? Not at all. Many scientists say that eating is an acquired habit like smoking and drinking, and that to live all we need to consume is air.

It was reported in 1936 that a woman named Bala Devi of Patrasayer in Bankura, India, had not taken food or water for 56 years. She did not urinate or defecate. She was 68 years old but looked like a child. Her only "food" was air.

The Bizarre Case of Wiley Brooks

For the last 18 years Wiley Brooks has not eaten anything at all and seldom takes fluids. He literally lives on air.

When Wiley was 28 years old and living in New York as a sound engineer, he felt as though his body and soul were deteriorating. "I realized I was a mess," he says. "My hair was falling out, I had a mild case of arthritis, and I was tired all the time. I wanted to stop the aging process. I looked into how the body works and became obsessed with it."

Brooks began his unusual program by cutting certain foods from his diet. He also indulged in a number of fasts. Finally, he decided that all food was bad for his system.

"When I stopped eating, my body started to get younger and stronger. Air is the most significant thing for man's survival. People should be placing an emphasis on cleaning up the air. After all, our food supply is dwindling."

Wiley feels that our diseases and ailments come from the poisons that accumulate in the blood stream through the process of eating. Says Wiley, "We think we will die if we don't eat, I see it completely the other way around. If I eat, I'll die."

He says that the body is an air machine and that it knows what to do. Cells regenerate themselves and the body will grow without food. All that is needed is oxygen, hydrogen, carbon and nitrogen. These, says Brooks, are the building blocks for all physical substance.

How then does he explain the fact that people do die of starvation? How does he explain the death of Bobby Sands, who fasted himself to death in Ireland? Not so surprisingly, Wiley has the answer.

"I don't recommend fasting. If you quit food cold turkey, your body starts eliminating toxins. When you stop eating, the toxins re-enter the bloodstream and poison you," Wiley tells us.

Sue Crawford, a nutritionist at Simon Fraser University's Department of Kinesiology, says that Brooks has most likely slowed down his metabolism but, physiologically, it is impossible to go without any liquids at all.

Crawford says, "You just can't rely on your body. There are no organisms in the biosphere that can go without substance. I think that what he is doing is interesting. Yogis have trained their boies to need less fuel, for example. But Brooks sounds like an anorexic."

Crawford continues, "My professor in England has something to say about this. 'Food kills, but not as fast as no food.' I think what Mr. Brooks is promoting is very risky."

Brooks calls his discipline "breatharianism." He operates a center in San Francisco where students are fed a transitional diet to purify the body—corn, fish, rice, chicken, and juices.

Brooks charges $300 for a five-day intensive study. He says, "The most important thing about becoming a breatharian is learning how the body works. The reference we have now is that the body must eat or it will die. From my viewpoint, if we do eat, we will die."

Dr. Michael Gerber, a Mill Valley, California physician who practices holistic medicine, is dubious. "It flies in the face of scientific knowledge of the Western variety. But stranger things are possible and have happened. I hate to rule out strange phenomena."

Although Wiley Brooks claims he does not take liquids, he will drink an occasional glass of lemon juice and water when he finds himself in a polluted urban environment. The mixture cleanses his system. He sleeps no more than seven hours a week, does no exercises. Despite his lack of food and exercise, he did back-lift 1,100 pounds on a television show, which indicates that he is certainly not weak. "I feel great," Brooks says. "I don't get sick. I don't have colds. I have ten times more energy than I had when I was eating." He's 47 years old, looks like 20. All he does for nourishment is breathe deeply.

When you live without food, Brooks says, "the body becomes absolutely perfectly healthy. And in a healthy body, a person becomes perfectly happy. Who on this planet needs more than perfect health and perfect happiness?" He is six feet tall and weighs 125 pounds.

How long does he expect to live? "Me? I'm shooting for the age 2,000!"

A Warning

It should be noted here that it is very dangerous to try Wiley Brooks' method. What's right for him may not be right for you. It's best at all times to consult your doctor before attempting any diet or period of fasting.

The Art of Breathing

While we can't endorse Wiley Brooks' method, we do feel he is on the right track in the area of proper breathing. Although it is possible to live without food or water for a month or six weeks, we cannot exist for more than a few minutes without breathing. The real tragedy is that very few of us breathe properly; and at times most of us forget to breathe at all! That sounds like a silly statement on the surface, but it's true. Our breathing becomes so shallow, especially when we're busy, that we don't incorporate sufficient oxygen into the system.

Deep breathing, therefore, is an absolute must. Once you have remembered to do so, you will find that your mind and body have been invigorated. You will be able to accomplish a great deal of physical and mental work without feeling exhausted.

According to medical science, all disease, including old age, originate with the impurities retained in the system. One of the most important factors in cleaning out these impurities is through proper breathing. Doing so insures one that the toxins in the system will not have an opportunity to accumulate.

How To Breath Properly

The lungs must be permitted to expand freely in every direction. Tight clothing tends to prevent this free expansion. Skin-tight jeans can act like a pair of bellows with the handles tied together. The wearer is choked at the waist, preventing proper lung expansion. Tight shirts and jackets will do the same. Correct posture is also important. When you are erect, whether standing, sitting, walking or working, your lungs can breathe properly; when you slouch you restrict your lungs unnecessarily.

Forming the habit of breathing deeply is easy. In no time you will discover that you can do it without any conscious effort on your part. What's more, you will find a bonus in the exercise in that you will experience fewer periods of the blues. This is a fact borne out by psychiatrists who, in many instances, ask their patients to spend a few moments breathing deeply before their couch sessions begin.

Should you decide to engage in the practice, it's best to do it outdoors. The air is fresher. A few moments a day should make a big difference in your outlook. Ideally, an hour would be fine, but not everyone can afford an hour in a busy day.

You can practice at your desk or workbench. You can sit erect and breathe deeply for a minute or two. When you stand, remember to stand up straight. When you're walking you can throw your shoulders back and take deep breaths of air.

We may not be ready to live on air, as Wiley Brooks does and Saint

Germain may have done, but we can make it work for us to a degree that we will feel stronger and healthier—and we may even shake the doldrums that occasionally assail us.

George Van Tassel and His "Time Machine"

In addition to Wiley Brooks, another unusual man claimed it was possible to virtually go on living forever. Back in the early 1950s, George Van Tassel had a series of contacts with a being who came out of a landed flying saucer and claimed he was from outer space. The communications usually took place in the wee hours while George camped outdoors near his trailer home on the desert, located 15 miles "as the crow flies" from the heart of Yucca Valley, California.

George, who has since passed away, maintained that his alien friend was very human in appearance and had only love in his heart toward the people of our planet. Though not a scientist, Van Tassel did have some technical shills, having been in aviation since the 1920s, and during the course of these other-worldly conversations (which were held via mental telepathy), information was given to him, which, the space person said, would enable mankind to build a circular building (which when properly equipped with the necessary technical instruments) to act as a "time machine" or rejuvenator. According to Van Tassel, anyone who passed through the doors of this circular structure which he called "Integratron" would have the aging process slowed down or retarded completely.

The Integratron was built according to specific instructions and stands ready to be put into use after some additional work has been completed. The Integratron has no metal parts in its construction, but the curious are told that it does house several electric gadgets, coils and instruments. Van Tassel's work has been continued at a reduced pace by his widow. Before his passing, however, George apparently was able to conduct a series of experiments in which he was able to increase the life span of mice from 72 to 223 days. It had been hoped that eventually similar tests could be carried out on human beings and the results would be just as positive, if not more so.

During the course of his experiments, the inventor reported that his activities were often monitored by government agents anxious to find out how his work was progressing. Apparently, not only were they interested in his supposed contacts with extraterrestrials, but in the Integratron which would certainly have tremendous repercussions on both the medical profession as well as society in general.

Unfortunately, we may never know just how valid this man's invention really is, as his contribution to science remains to be seen until the time when someone else can proceed where he left off.

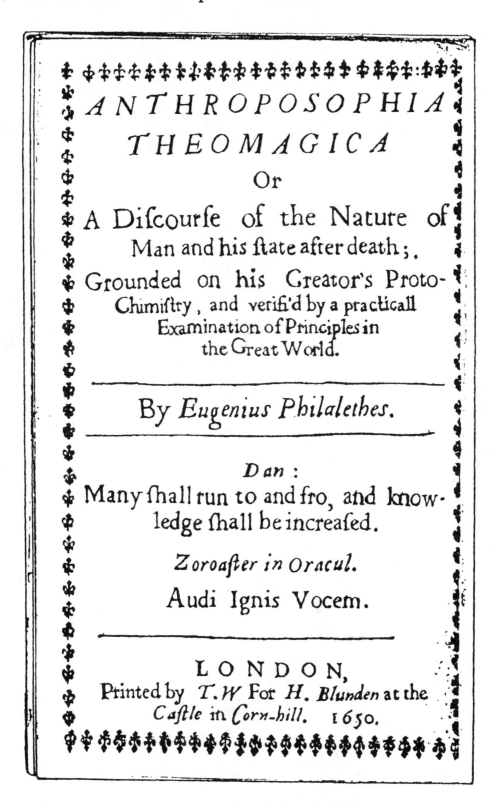

A rare alchemy text printed in London in 1650.

Wiley Brooks has appeared numerous times in the media where he claims to have gone without eating for nearly 20 years. He believes this has enabled him to stay healthy and youthful.

The Lure of Death

You may think that this heading is ridiculous. How can death have a lure? Don't we always try to avoid it? True, but there are times when we may succumb to the lure because we don't have any alternative.

Albert Heim, a Swiss geologist, wrote a report on the subject of dying in 1892. It was published in *Omega,* a journal devoted to the psychological aspects of the subject. The report is one of the best collections of sudden death experiences ever assembled. Heim interviewed about 30 survivors of Alpine falls after he himself nearly died in a similar accident.

Strangely, Heim's report remained buried for years. It wasn't until the early 1970s that Russell Noyes, Jr. came upon it and had it translated into English. Noyes is a psychiatrist with the University of Iowa and was conducting his own research into the strange lure that comes to victims who are on the brink of sudden death. His conclusion was that the experience of dying is broken down into three phases. They are resistance, life review and transcendence.

During the first phase of the individual fights against forces that are insurmountable, which are the external dangers. They might be falling, drowning, or suffering from the outrages of horrible violence against him. When he realizes that he cannot survive, he finds himself succumbing to a strange longing to surrender to death. At this point his fears dissolve and he welcomes death.

The second phase, the life review, is described by Noyes as possibly being an emotional defense against extinction. When there is no future, the victim will concentrate on the happy times of the past.

When Albert Heim had his near-death experience he said later, "I saw myself as a seven-year-old boy going to school then in the fourth grade classroom with my beloved teacher Weisz. I acted out my life as though I were on a stage upon which I looked down from the highest gallery in the theater. My sisters, and especially my wonderful mother, who was so important to me, were all around me.

"Death through falling is subjectively very pleasant. Those who have died in the mountains have, in their last moments, reviewed their individual pasts in states of transfiguration. Elevated above corporeal grief, they were under the sway of noble and profound thoughts, heavenly music, and a feeling of peace and reconciliation. They fell through a blue and roseate, magnificent heaven; then everything was suddenly still."

Literary patron Caresse Crosby remembered her near drowning when she was seven. "I saw the efforts to bring me back to life and I tried not to come back. I was a carefree child, yet that moment in my life has never been equalled for pure happiness."

The Death Hormone

After the Pacific salmon deposit their eggs they die. What actually kills them is a flood of adrenocorticotrophic hormone. The theory that nature becomes indifferent to us after procreation may be true. As we grow older our immune system, our main life of defense against disease, falls into a decline. The antibodies produced by the specialized white cells become weak and almost useless.

The process that kills the Pacific salmon is also at work in our bodies, only far less dramatically. This is the opinion of Dr. W. Donner Denckla of the Harvard Medical School. In the early 1970s he worked with old rats at the Roche Institute of Molecular Biology in Nutley, New Jersey. He learned that although levels of thyroid hormones remain almost unchanged in old rats, the responsiveness of their tissue to the hormones declines to about one-third of the youthful value. Dr. Denckla saw evidence that this is also true in old humans. Even though the aged have plenty of thyroid hormone,s the hormones don't appear to do their assigned tasks.

Dr. Denckla's theory is that there is a death hormone secreted by the pituitary gland which decreases the receptivity to thyroid hormones. His experiments on rats apparently confirm it. When he underfed the rodents there was a severe decrease in output of the pituitary hormones. He also discovered that when the pituitary is removed from old rats, the animals regain some of their youthful physiology.

When the pituitary glands were removed from the rats, they were given throxine, the principal thyroid hormone. The rodents showed a remarkable rejuvenation. Removing the pituitary apparently shuts off the death hormone flow.

Dr. Denckla says that there is a death agent in our bodies. So far he has not found it, but he says: "Finding the death hormone will be the first step toward creating a drug to block the action. If we can reproduce the immune competence of a ten year old—when man is at his healthiest — your expected life span will go to 200, 300, even 400 years. That's what we will be dealing with in the next century."

Did Saint Germain Have His Pituitary Removed?

We don't know. We don't know that medical science was aware of the gland in the 16th century. Had he discovered the drug that effectively neutralized the death hormone? If he had, he managed to keep the discovery a dark secret. For all we know, the elixirs he took religiously may have contained the elusive drug.

At any rate, we would not advise anyone to have his or her pituitary gland removed on the chance that it might prolong life. We would not presume to offer medical advice here. Questions concerning your body should always be asked only of your doctor.

Why Do We Want To Die?

Incredible as it sounds, some of us actually do want to die. This fact was brought out by Dr. Arnold A. Hutschnecker in his book, *The Will to Live*. He wrote:

We select our own illness. We choose our time to die... We die only when we are ready to die. We die when we want to die. If we truly have the incentive to live—if we have something to live for—then no matter how sick we may be, no matter how close to death, we do not die. We live because we want to live. It is not the 'everything we live for' in the eyes of the world which keeps us alive, but the something which meets our uncompromising measure of what is worth living for... To live long, not only in years but in the enjoyment of them, we must understand and control the forces which shorten life. Both early and late, we must take the time to cultivate the will to live.

The Will to Die—A Deep Mystery

This negative force is the most mysterious of all human failings. It is as powerful as the positive force which keeps us alive. During the Korean War psychiatrists were astounded by the give-up-itis that afflicted some American prisoners of war. Discouraged by their confinement in North Korean camps, cold, hungry, and lonely, some GIs simply went to their cots, rolled over and died. Physically, nothing was wrong with them. Undoubtedly, they were emotional basket cases, and they selected their time to die.

Most of us know of people who are sick, who could get well if they wanted to, but refuse to. They are unaware of their self-destructiveness because they have successfully hidden the truth from themselves. Some tend to be illness repeaters. Employers generally know that the same group of employees will be absent due to sickness. Doctors know that illness can be produced by nagging and by suggestion.

Dr. D.M. Kissen of Scotland's Health Department once devised a questionnaire to be answered by patients at a diagnostic chest clinic. The survey revealed that emotional factors such as unhappiness in the home and the deprivation of love preceded the onset of pulmonary tuberculosis. Many patients in the United States who go to doctors with a great variety of physical complaints are really cases of depression in disguise. And there are some cases of arthritis which can be traced to resentment.

Be Happy—And Live Longer

Being happy was certainly one of Saint Germain's traits. Descriptions of him by various individuals of rank who knew him agree that he was a happy human being. He worked hard at this jobs, but his outlook on life was also rosy. His spirits and joy of living were always high. One important secret he shared willingly was that he was interested in a great many things. He had an enormous will to live, which means nothing more than staying active and believing that long life will follow.

The *New England Journal of Medicine* recently completed an incredible study. Researchers spent 40 years probing the overall mental health and medical condition of 188 men. The subjects were given yearly or biannual questionnaires. They underwent extensive interviews at ages 30 and 47.

In 1967, psychiatrists rated 57 of the men as being mentally healthy. In 1975, 97 percent of these same men were rated in excellent health. Each rating was made by a doctor unaware of the man's previous mental and physical state. Dr. George Vaillant, a Harvard University psychologist, who coordinated the study, said that the results support the old saying, "Be happy, you'll live longer."

The study showed that men who were of good humor and had many social contacts remained healthy. Those who were unhappy in their marriages, their jobs, and their leisure time were subject to chronic health problems. The healthy men said that they kept active and enjoyed being with other people. They also said that they never kept jobs in which the stress levels were too high, or if they found no enjoyment in the work. All had hobbies, some of them juggling three or four at the same time.

7,000 Americans Puzzle Scientists

All of them are over the age of 100. Scientists admit that they don't know why these people have lived so long. Bernard Strehler, professor of biology at the University of Southern California and president of the Association for the Advancement of Aging Research, says the mystery may be solved in another generation. When the breakthrough comes, people will live decades longer than they do now.

At present, scientists are successful with laboratory animals. Here, they can prolong youthful vigor and extend life, but they still haven't hit on the secret that will permit humans to live into their second century.

Research scientists feel that in the field of aging we are controlled by our biological clocks. Like it or not, we have a fixed span of life, like everything else in nature. The May fly lives for a day. A dog lives for about 15 years. Humans experience body changes at fixed periods. We all walk and talk at about the same ages. We experience puberty in our early teens. Menopause occurs always in women between the age of 40 and 50. Why these things happen at certain times was discovered by microbiologist Leonard Hayflick of Stanford University. In 1961 he was engaged in cancer research at Wister Institute in Philadelphia. He learned that fibroblast cells, one of the main components of most body tissues, are apparently programmed to die. His research showed that the trillions of cells in our body, with the exception of muscle and brain cells, are constantly dividing and renewing themselves. One cell splits and becomes two cells. These cells are kept within definite limits by physical wear and tear, which destroys most of them.

Hayflick took cells from embryos and aborted fetuses and discovered that they divided vigorously in the beginning but then died at a point around the 50th division. Cells from young adults divided about 30 times before dying. Cells from mature adults died after the 20th division or so.

Hayflick froze some cells and managed to stop the clock on them. As soon as they thawed, however, the clock started again and the cells started dividing as they had before being frozen.

The microbiologist discovered that the number of times a cell is divided is closely related to the life-span of the species. A mouse lives for about three years. Its cells doubled only 12 times. A chicken, which can live for about 30 years, has cells that double 25 times.

We must assume that there is a genetic master plan for us, too, and we don't have any control over it. Mayflick says our biological clock is wound for about 110 to 120 years because that's about how long it takes for our cells to double the maximum of about 50 times.

Activity—The Secret of a Long Life

Are you an energy person? You've seen them. You may even work with them. As they grow older they appear to gather more energy than when they were young. They always have enough energy to do the job—with plenty left over. They are always full of plans for the future right up to the very end of their lives.

For example, George Washington wrote a 6,000 word article on the importance of rotating crops only a few days before he died. Titian was 85 when he painted his greatest masterpieces, one of them being of Saint Germain. He lived to be 99. Oliver Wendell Holmes was 79 when he started writing *Over the Teacups*. Sophocles wrote *Oedipus at Colonus* shortly before he died at 90.

All of these people were doers and planners. They lived a long time because they wanted to. Their energy was boundless. They had work to do and they wanted to finish it.

The Amazing Dr. Lillian J. Martin

This woman lived to nearly 100 years. She was a high school chemistry teacher to the age of 65, when she retired. At that point she made some plans for the future—and carried them out! In the 1930s she went to Germany for a few years to learn about a new science called psychology. She then took a professorship at Stanford University and, during her tenure, contributed ten new concepts to psychological research.

Dr. Martin had already had a full life at age 65, but instead of sitting back to await death, she remained active. Her head was full of ideas and plans. Her theory was that you don't remain young by living in the past. The thing to do was to always search for new things to do. In her case, doing something new embraced child guidance work. This was a new field and she felt she had something to contribute to it. Dr. Martin opened the first mental-hygiene clinic for preschool children in San Francisco.

In this line of work she came into contact with parents and grandparents. Dr. Martin was not happy with what was happening to the grandparents she saw. They seemed to be going downhill fast. Something had to be done for them. Their interest in life had to be renewed. She opened an old-age clinic in San Francisco. Soon, clinics sprang up in Los Angeles and New York City.

The amazing Dr. Martin never stopped learning. At 65 she learned how to type. In her 70s she learned how to drive a car. At 75 she took a trip to Russia—alone. At 81 she toured Mexico in her car—alone. Dr. Martin was 88 when she toured South America. That trip included a journey up the Amazon.

One year after she returned, Dr. Martin took over the management of a 65-acre farm. Her farm hands were four 60-year-old men.

Another Go-Getter—Dr. Lillian M. Gilbreth

When this woman was in her 70s, the National Institute of Social Sciences awarded her a gold medal for distinguished services to humanity. She was an engineer, psychologist, and a professor. She had mothered 18 children, authored ten books and received nine academic degrees. Dr. Gilbreth was also the industrial consultant for her own corporation.

Were these people blessed with a secret source of energy? Not likely. What made them stand out was that they had a fierce desire to live. They loved life. They loved what they were doing, and were in love with learning. They forgot their ages, they did not live in the past, and they stayed active.

A Philosophy of Life

You have a philosophy even if you don't think you do. We rarely express it in so many words. We live it. If you don't think you have one, then why not try this one on for size?

This philosophy is simply being your best. You might like to feel your best and look your best. When you exert an effort, you will want it to be your best effort. We can't always make the world safer, saner, or happier, but what we can do is make ourselves feel better by doing the best we can with what we've got.

Add to that the need to control your own life. You will insist on making your own decisions about what you will do with your life. You won't be led by those into areas that don't really interest you.

Learn to love what you do. Successful people will freely admit that they love the job, profession, trade or whatever it is they do because they love to do it.

St. Germain's Philosophy

St. Germain is a good example of this love of doing what interests one. He was deeply interested in all of the sciences and was a master at most of them, especially alchemy. He was an art expert because he loved great works of art. He was a music lover, but more than that he was a master at the violin. He was extremely interested in literature. In fact, many scholars believe that as Francis Bacon, Saint Germain was the author of all of the Shakespeare plays.

The story goes that when Francis Bacon was a young lawyer he wrote the plays and gave them to William Shakespeare, who was an actor. Shakespeare signed his name to the plays, taking the credit for what Bacon (Saint Germain) had done.

All you need do is examine the philosophies of Bacon and Shakespeare to understand why one never died and the other passed away at the age of 50.

Bacon was a man of learning. He was well versed in matters of statesmanship, in court etiquette, history, in law, in navigation, in philosophy, in foreign languages, in natural science, held revolutionary views on medicine, was keenly interested in psychology and was a student of the Bible.

On the other hand, according to researchers, Shakespeare was interested in none of these things, or anything else, for that matter. Records show that he was uneducated, a drunkard and profligate. Pope called him a "man of no education." Voltaire called him a "drunken savage." There are only six known examples of Shakespeare's handwriting in existence and all of them show one who was not used to holding a pen.

The lesson here is obvious: To live long, one must acquire many interests. Investigate. Probe new areas. Don't be afraid to tackle fields you've never thought about before. Chances are you'll find new delights. All of the people mentioned here were not born with the knowledge they had; they had to acquire it. There is no reason why you can't do the same. In your own way, you can be another Francis Bacon, or Dr. Gilbreth or Dr. Martin. All you have to do is exert the effort—and make it your best effort.

Are You Old?

The New York State Join Legislative Committee on the problems of aging drew up a list of attitudes which are good tip-offs. The Committee says you are old if:

You feel old.

You feel that you have learned all you need to learn.

You find yourself saying, "I'm too old for that."

You feel that tomorrow holds no promise.

You find no amusement in youth's fun; their banter irks you.

You would rather talk than listen.

You long for the good old days; you are sure they were the best.

You won't help your friends, neighbors, community.

You have no plans for tomorrow.

You would rather win an argument than be right.

To live long, not only in years, but in the enjoyment of them, means that you must understand and control the forces that shorten life. If you don't have the will to live, then it must be developed no matter what your age.

The Right Mental Attitude

If you were to ask a group of long livers what their secret was, chances ar they would tell you that feeling good mentally played a big part in it. The right mental attitude is vitally important.

There was a woman in Kansas City who was 102 and had no idea how she'd managed it. She told a reporter, "I suppose it's just that I've managed to chance with the times."

But it was more than that. She had gone to college, married a minister and then, in 1921, became associate director of the Presbyterian student center at the University of Kansas. She lived near the campus, attending gatherings of two women's groups and a literary club. She went to a beauty parlor once a week. She said, once, "I'm the busiest woman in town. I can't wait to get up in the morning."

The clue to her longevity is in what she said, "I'm the busiest woman in town." She was busy with her work. It was not the frantic, back-to-the-wall type of work, but work that kept her active. Work as opposed to idleness. Work as opposed to watching television, when the mind is not expanding, when a book is not read, and an interest not pursued.

Saint Germain Was a Worker

All the research on this enigmatic character shows that he was a steady, productive worker. Although he had enough riches to remain idle for the rest of his life, he chose to work, to help others (remember his charities to the poor), and to improve his mind.

Work and Rest, the Necessary Balance

Learn to recognize fatigue for what it is, which is not the result of hard work but of undue stress, tension and wasted effort. We need to know how to concentrate our forces so that we don't work in an aimless manner. Use only the force necessary to accomplish a task. Cultivate the art of working gracefully. Avoid unnecessary strain. Work should be invigorating, and then followed by restful sleep. You do need to rest, too, to take out time to sit quietly, to read, to enjoy a board game, or to just close your eyes and find inner peace.

"Letting go" after a hard days' work is important. Too many of us take the job home with us and mentally repeat everything we did all day. Actually, this bad habit can be more fatiguing than the actual day's work. Some of us talk about the work to friends, thereby reliving every detail. If you're going to do that, you might as well go back to work and put in another full shift (and get paid for it).

The Art of Relaxing

If you were to relax fully, the way a child does, you would acquire enough rest in a few minutes to put in another few hours of work without fatigue. Unfortunately, very few of us have the knack. We lost it growing up. But it can be regained through conscious effort. All we need do is to relax our muscles. Let the tension ooze out of them. Remain perfectly still. Stay in a semi-darkened room and think quiet thoughts. If you can, watch how a child relaxes in bed. Watch him stretch and find a comfortable position. Then see how quickly he falls asleep. Best to do it surreptitiously; if he is aware of you he might want to stay awake and talk.

Work Keeps You Young

"Leisure is something that you want to do that is of no use to anybody. I'm not impressed. I dislike the idea of leisure very much. I think a person should live."

Those sage words were spoken by the late anthropologist Margaret

Mead. Dr. Heinz Woltereck said that if there is a secret to prolonged life it is work. He says that the only way to keep organs healthy and active is by using them, and he cites an experiment in which identical twins were studied. One was given work to do. The other was allowed to remain idle. At the end of the experiment the organs and muscles of the twins were examined. The general health of both was evaluated. The worker's health had improved. The idler's health had deteriorated.

You know from your own experience that when you are engaged in work you enjoy you have no time for restlessness, boredom or self-pity. You have also known people with inquiring minds and have thought about how great it is to be interested in so many things. Wonder no more! Find your own areas of interests and keep your mind as active as you can.

Herbert Hoover once said: "I've always been able to find new jobs that proved infinitely more satisfying than sitting around. When I'm loafing I get tired of myself. Work is the stuff that satisfies—that makes you feel useful and worthwhile.

"I've known people who have retired from work and I've been bored by a good many of them. Without work to occupy their minds they turn to reminiscing and talking about their ills and pills. It's not long before they start falling apart. An oldster who keeps working—even if it's only part time work—has something worth talking about.

"It's my philosophy that folks should never retire from all work. If they do there's a good chance they will shrivel into a nuisance to all mankind!"

When the former President made those remarks to a newsman he was 86. What he was striving to say was that we should not become workaholics, but that we should have something to do so that we have a reason for getting out of bed every day.

Our Mysterious Subconscious

Your subconscious is an amazing entity. It will do your bidding without question. For instance, if you tell it you would like to get up tomorrow morning at 6:00 a.m., it will wake you.

As great as your subconscious is, it is also a loaded gun. The problem is that it acts blindly. Feed it negative thoughts and it will act accordingly; load it up with positive thinking and your whole life changes for the good.

The subconscious doesn't really care where the suggestion comes from, whether it be advertising, hypnotism or autosuggestion, it will accept the thought and act upon it.

Your Subconscious Can Keep You Moving

Psychiatrists say it is possible to suggest to yourself that you are young and healthy and, in doing so, see an amazing transformation take place. Instead of concentrating on old age and disease, replace them with thoughts of youth and health. You've heard of the person who said, "All I did was think thin, and I was thin." Why can't we apply that same thought process to thinking young and healthy? One noted psychiatrist said: "A careful study of the lives of fortunate people reveals that they let nothing dim their hopes, interests, loves, nor allowed anything to stand in the way of the fulfillment of these primary longings.

"When you and I realize this fact and also apply it, our personal lives become transformed whatever our problems may be. This is the way to mental health and a return to the spirit of youth."

The Power of Prayer

Prayer is an intangible entity. It works, but we know little about it. The subject has never been fully explored, which is rather incredible. We can find plenty of examples to show that prayer works, and we can point to people like Charles Steinmetz, the electrical genius of the General Electric Company, who said that the next realm of research would be the spiritual, and the next field that of prayer.

His prediction hasn't come true yet, but Dr. Norman Vincent Peale said, "Prayer is the greatest power in the world. It is a pity that more people do not know how to use it."

Experiment Proves That Prayer Works

Some time ago Reverend Franklin Loehr decided to find out once and for all if prayer really worked. He was a chemist as well as a theologian, and his experiment consisted of a series of tests on living plants at the Religious Research Foundation, Inc.

Altogether, Rev. Loehr conducted 700 experiments. A total of 27,000 seeds and seedlings were used, and more than 100,000 measurements were taken. Six other experimental groups supplemented and corroborated the reverend's work.

Dr. Loehr's results indicate that a thought is a thing, meaning that the brain emits waves strong enough to be measured and graphed. One group among his 150 assistants prayed to God that their seeds would be successful and healthy. Another group made no such plea to God. The seeds that were prayed over grew three to four times faster than those which received no prayer.

If prayer works well on seeds, why not us? Spiritual aid is there for the asking. It works no matter what your religious persuasion is. After all, didn't we start as seeds?

Although we will pray for good health and longevity, we must remember that in our prayers the phrase must always be: "Not my will, but Thine will be done."

Five Steps to Tap the Power of Prayer

1. Relax. The room should be dark, or semi-dark, and you should be alone and with no distractions.

2. Accept or "turn on" the power of prayer, which can be had for the asking. This ability increases with practice.

3. Direct the power to what you want accomplished. This, too, will take a bit of practice because our minds tend to wander.

4. Visualize it as you want it to be. In this case we want good health and vigor into old age. Picture yourself as being healthy and vigorous even though, in your mind's eye, you may be well up in years.

5. Give thanks that it is being accomplished. We give thanks all the time to those who do small favors for us, why not extend our thanks to God for the biggest favor He can bestow on anyone—good health?

The Importance of Faith

Dr. Carl Jung once said, "In all the thousands who come to me for help, those who have some faith, some religion, get well more quickly."

Mature people are spiritual people. That doesn't mean that they follow a particular religion, but they do have faith in themselves and in others. They are aware of the fact that there is a power greater than themselves and that the universe has a purpose as well as order.

These People Lived Long Lives

Captain John Diamond

In 1902, Captain Jack Diamond of San Francisco reached the age of 107. At that time he taught a class in physical culture and personally demonstrated the exercises. He also walked 20 miles a day without undue fatigue. His outlook was always bright. Captain Diamond never overate and made sure at all times that he ate only food that was nourishing. How long did he live? That question cannot be answered because the records of his birth and death were burned in a fire.

Zaro Agha

This man died on June 29, 1934. He was 164 years old. He worked in Istanbul as a porter for more than 100 years and became a father for the last time at age 90.

Thomas Parr

Parr lived through ten reigns of English monarchs. He was born in the parish of Alberbury, in Shropshire, England. When he died on November 13, 1635, he was reputed to be 152. For the most part he was a simple peasant, but during his later years he gained a measure of fame. His portraits were painted by Rubens and Vandyke. He was presented at the court of Charles I, and was buried in Westminster Abbey.

Mahmud Eivazov

The Soviets claimed that this man was 150 years old in 1958. We don't know if he is still living. What we do know is that he was a resident of Azerbaijan, a Caucasian republic in the U.S.S.R., that he had one daughter aged 123 and three sons who were centenarians.

Mohammed Khalil Abdul Hawa

This Jerusalem resident celebrated his 136th birthday in 1957. It was said of him that he was the oldest man in the Middle East.

Gabriel Sanchez

At last report this man at the age of 135 was the oldest person in the Valley of Vilcabamba, in southeastern Ecuador. Gabriel attracted the attention of a group of scientists researching longevity. Allegedly, he is still active, still farming, an occupation he claimed he pursued for 120 years.

Michael Watkins

Watkins came to America from Liberia as a slave when he was 12 years old. He was renamed Charles Smith by a rancher who owned him. At any rate, he celebrated his 134th birthday on July 4, 1976, and was considered the oldest man in the United States.

Khfaf Lasuria

The Soviets claim to have another long liver in Khfaf Lasuria, who lived in the Soviet republic of Abkhasia. This man was a member of a troupe of performers and was still dancing at the age of 131 (1972).

Gabriel Erazo

Another resident of the Vilcabamba Valley in Ecuador. In this area, one person out of every 100 claims to be a centenarian. In 1973, at the age of 130, Erazo was still putting in a full day's work in his garden.

Osman Bzheniya

Still another Russian, this one from the village of Lykhny in Abkhasia, in the U.S.S.R. Osman was still working part time on his farm in 1973 at the age of 120.

Tatzumbie Dupea

This long liver was a Paiute Indian born near Pine Hills in California in 1849. His name means "Beautiful Star." Dupea died in February 1970, making him 120 years old.

Chief Red Cloud

He also lived to be 120 years old. The Sioux died at Steubenville in the fall of 1962. As a young man he traveled with Buffalo Bill's Wild West Show.

Mrs. Harry Harrison Moran

The last time anyone checked, and that was in March 1974, this woman was still receiving a pension from the government because her husband died in the Civil War. At that time she was 118 years old and was the oldest surviving widow of a veteran of that war.

George Fruits

George fought in the American Revolution and died at Alamo, Indiana, on August 6, 1876. He was 114 years old.

Mrs. Delina Filkens

This Herkimer County, New York resident had birth records to prove her advanced age. She died on December 4, 1928 at age 113 years.

Caesar Paul

The oldest Canadian, an Algonquin Indian, died in Pembroke, Ontario, on July 25, 1975, at the age of 112 years.

St. Germain, The Champion Long Liver

Al of the people mentioned above certainly held some secrets to long life, but so far no one has topped the old master St. Germain. He is still alive. There is no record of his death. If we can believe the stories, he is teaching in the Himalayas, and often travels to Shangri-La, said to be a gateway to the inner earth.

Transcaucasia

The area is located at the Soviet Union's southernmost point. It's called Soviet Georgia. The section is 750 miles long with a population of 9.5 million. The boast here is that they have the highest number of long-lived people than anywhere else in the world. They may be right. A census taken in 1970 of the entire region showed that there were 5,000 people who were 100 years old or older.

No other region in the world has been studied so thoroughly. Researchers have compiled tremendous documentation. Recently, two doctors in Tbilisi, the capital of Georgia, studied 15,000 people in the Caucasus. All were over 80. The doctors were Professor G.E. Pitzkhelauri, director of the Gerontology Center, and his assistant Dr. Deli Dzhorbenadze. They also examined 700 people who were 100 years old or older.

The subjects were asked to show their birth certificates or baptismal records. Many did. They were also questioned about historical events, dates of marriages, births of children, and so on. The facts were checked and the doctors were able to confirm that the people told the truth. Outside gerontologists have since visited the area and have corroborated the Russians' findings.

Each subject was given a physical examination. The doctors were amazed at the results. Nearly all were given clean bills of health.

The Incredible Shirali "Baba" Mislimov

Shirali was from the area described above. His nickname, "Baba," means baby. He was the forbearer of five living generations. In 1870 he planted an orchard and continued to tend it until his death. He remembered incidents during the Crimean War (1853–1856). When he died, his widow was 120 years old. They had been married for 102 years. Baba died in 1973. He was 168 years old.

The facts on this case were documented by Dr. Abdulla I. Karayev, head of the Department of Physiology at Azerbayan's Academy of Sciences.

Tsurba The Amazing Long Liver

Tsurba was 160 years old when she died. A Russian reporter who witnessed her death said she "withered away like an old tree." Tsurba did not begin to shrink until she was 140. Twenty years later she was only three feet tall. She slept in a baby's crib, and that was where she died.

The facts in this case and in Baba's were verified by outside researchers.

What Secrets Lie in Transcaucasia?

Oddly enough, many of the places in this region are tourist meccas. Russians flock to Sochi and Sukhumi on the Black Sea. Some go to Baku on the Caspian Sea. Many tourists take "the water cure," which is merely bathing in the sea. Some take the "grape cure," which means eating nothing but the sweet grapes of Georgia. The mineral waters in this area are supposed to be the best anywhere on the continent. In fact, the boiled water of Borzhom is exported to cities all over Russia and even to foreign ports.

But you won't find the centenarians in these resort spas. They live in the foothills, where life is rougher. Much of the Soviet Union's tobacco, tea and citrus fruits are grown here and the inhabitants work hard to get the produce to market.

Their secret of long life is in their diet and their ability to keep active.

The Caucasian Diet

Residents of Soviet Georgia are fond of cheese and buttermilk. They eat lots of green onions, tomatoes, cucumbers, beans, and cabbage. They also eat beef, chicken, young goat, and fruit. They consume between 1,700 and 1,900 calories a day.

They do not eat bread and potatoes the way other Russians do. But they do bake two-foot-long loaves of unleavened bread which is crisp and served hot. They also bake a bread substitute called abusta, a corn-meal mash cooked in water without salt. They eat it with their fingers and dip it into various sauces. Most Caucasians like their food spicy; they use red peppers, black pepper, garlic and pomegranate juice.

There are 50,000 people in Abkhazia who are over 80 years old. Many of them are Muslims, so they don't drink alcohol. They do, however, drink a wine that they produce themselves. They have it at lunch and dinner. They grow tobacco, but don't usually smoke it. Russian scientists say that because these people drink so much buttermilk and other sour milk products, and because they eat pickled vegetables and drink wine, they effectively arrest the development of arteriosclerosis.

Even in Death They Look Young

Georgians usually have their own teeth until death. They have luxuriant hair and good eyesight, erect postures, and have never had serious illness. They have good hearing right up to the end. Dr. Samuel Rosen of Mount Sinai Hospital in New York visited the area in 1970 and attributed the residents' good hearing to the diet of unsaturated fats and large quantities of fruits and vegetables.

No Fatties in Georgia

Fat people are rare in Caucasia. Overeating is just not done. Everything that is eaten is burned up through almost constant activity.

The people here expect to live a long time, and they do. They are actually programmed to live long. They have parents, grandparents and great-grandparents who are alive, healthy and vital human beings. They know that there is no reason why they, too, can't live long.

And no matter how old they become, they almost enjoy the feeling of being useful. The older they grow the more respected they become. Younger people turn to them for wisdom and guidance.

Is St. Germain in Vilcabamba Valley, Ecuador?

If a man wanted to prolong his life indefinitely, the place to live might be Vilcabamba Valley. At least two of the world's longest livers, Gabriel Sanchez (120) and Gabriel Erazo (130) came from this section of the world. In 1969, Dr. Miguel Salvador, president of Ecuador's Society of Cardiologists, took eight doctors to Vilcabamba and thoroughly examined 628 extremely old people.

He learned that men in their 90s were still plowing fields with younger men. Women of the same age were still gathering strands of sheep or working in bakeries. Other old men stood all day in a muddy ooze to make adobe bricks.

The most astonishing discovery of all was the almost total absence of serious diseases. Heart ailments, for instance, were almost unheard of. Today, Vilcabamba is known as the "island of immunity," or the "island of health and longevity."

The Mystery of Vilcabamba

There are curative powers in this valley, yet no one is quite sure what they are or how they exist. The fact is that these powers, whatever they are, might be beyond the ken of medical knowledge.

A case in point is an American named Albert Kramer who had a heart ailment. He went to Vilcabamba, rented an adobe farmhouse and stayed a year. His recovery was miraculous. He experienced what doctors termed a "cardiological compensation," or a spontaneous improvement in his heart condition.

Vilcabambans Are Healthy People

The average intake of calories is 1,200 a day, about half of what we consume in the United States. They eat an ounce of meat a week. Their diet consists mostly of grain, soup, corn, yucca root, beans, potatoes, oranges and bananas. They make a soup called Repe out of bananas, beans, cheese, salt and lard. Vilcabambans don't use much sugar, and what they do use is unrefined. When asked how they have managed to live so long they will usually say it is the herb tea they drink. Scientists don't agree.

Their Surprising Hang-ups

Vilcabambans smoke and drink rather heavily. Oldsters drink two to four cups of rum a day. They smoke 40 to 60 cigarettes a day. Many are hooked on strong coffee. A woman who claims to be 104 drinks five cups of coffee a day.

Why Do They Live So Long?

Doctors who have studied the people and the area say that Vilcabambans live to ripe old ages because they have regular work habits, frugal diets, and have a good climate. The people go to bed at sunset and rise at dawn. They are always active. The air they breathe is pure. They have no stressful situations.

Of course, they do catch cold, have attacks of asthma and arthritis. When that happens they see their medicine man, who uses cocoa leaves as a remedy. If they suffer stiffness and pain, they will walk two miles to Sunungo and take a mineral spring bath.

People Who Live 150 Years

To see these people you have to go to Hunza, which is at the top of the world in Pakistan. Hunza country is a paradise 200 miles long and a mile wide. It's completely enclosed by mountain peaks, some of which are 25,000 feet high. The Hunzakuts live an average of 150 years.

Far-fetched? Author Renee Taylor, in her book, *Hunza Health Secrets for Long Life and Happiness,* wrote: "In Hunza, people manage to live to over 100 years of age in perfect mental and physical health... men of 90 are new fathers and women of 50 still conceive."

Hunzakuts Never Get Old

It is not unusual to see men of 90 and 100 still herding sheep and goats in the summer. They do a lot of climbing. Most of their arable land is on mountain slopes. A typical farmer might have to climb a thousand feet several times a day. They all drink from the Hunza River, which is rich in minerals.

The life is slow and stress-free. Everybody works. Bedtime is sunset and all rise at dawn. No one gets "old" in Hunza. There are "young years," "middle years," and "rich years."

In 1897 the beautiful Emma Calve, a famous Parisian entertainer, autographed a photo of her friend Count St. Germain "the great chiromancer
who has told me many truths."

Diet—It's Importance In Long Life

Not long ago an author named Arnold De Vries wrote a book titled *Primitive Man and His Food*. In it he made a strong point on the importance of diet in the primitive man's world. His research indicated that so long as the native diet was adhered to, the tribe flourished. De Vries studied North and South American Indians, Europeans, Asians, Africans, Australian aborigines, New Zealand Maoris, and other tribes. He said that all of them had bright and perfect teeth. Eyes were clear and strong. They had incredible endurance and could run all day without becoming fatigued. Diseases were rare. Wounds healed rapidly. A woman could bear a perfect baby in about a half hour and without pain. An hour later she could be back in the fields at work. Most people, barring accidents, lived to be 100. There was no sign of degeneration, no loss of sight or hearing, and no gray hair.

Why? Diet. The food eaten by these tribes was fresh, wholesome and natural. Some tribes were vegetarians, some were lacto-vegetarians, and some were big meat eaters. Still others were consumers of dairy products. In every case, however, the food was fresh, wholesome and much of it raw. And as long as each tribe stuck to what it was used to eating, its members were strong and healthy.

So what does that tell us?

Our Diet is Killing Us

Yes, it's true. The best proof lies with those same tribes mentioned above. When civilization encroached on these primitive people, their health went into a sharp decline. They were given canned and refined food. White sugar and white flour became part of their daily intake. It was then that health problems developed. Their teeth decayed. Diseases attacked children and adults. Childbirth became diffiicult and prolonged. The natives were no longer energetic for long periods and many of them

80

showed early signs of old age. Death came earlier.

So there is no mystery about why we die earlier than those rugged tribesmen. Our diet is such a disgrace it's a wonder we live out our three score and ten.

It is actually killing us.

Proof That Diet (The Right Kind) Can Keep Us Alive

During the First World War Denmark was in serious trouble. There was a frightful food shortage. It was so severe that it produced malnutrition throughout the country. Actually, Denmark faced starvation.

The government knew of only one man who was capable of handling the problem. His name was Mikkel Hindhede, Superintendent of the Danish State Institute of Food Research.

The first thing Hindhede did was to set up new food regulations. Pork and other foods were eliminated completely. So were alcoholic beverages. He was not opposed to drinking, but grain was too precious to waste on alcohol. He insisted that bread be made the right way, with whole-meal flours, eye, oats and bran. He made sure that such items as green vegetables, fruits, milk, and butter were available and that the people consume them every day.

From March 1917 to the end of the war, Denmark became the healthiest nation in Europe. In only one year, the death rate fell more than 40 percent. That was the lowest figure ever registered in any country. There were no cases of malnutrition and diseases were almost unheard of. The influenza epidemic, which devastated Europe and the United States, barely touched Denmark.

Why? Diet. The right food. It's as simple as that. Hindhede held no magic formula. He simply knew that what his people ate were the wrong things, and that to turn the situation around he needed only to bring in supplies of the foods that make for good health.

Here's More Proof

The incident occurred during the outbreak of World War II. The area was Cheshire County, England. Doctors knew something was wrong in this section of England when draft registrants revealed that they were in horrendous shape. The young men were so appallingly unhealthy that the physicians in Cheshire County drafted a "Medical Testament" in which they announced that something had to be done to improve the population's health.

A diet was worked out by these concerned doctors. It was designed for pregnant women. The first item on the agenda was bread. It had to be made with whole-wheat flour and reinforced with half its weight in raw wheat germ. The flour had to be freshly ground and within 36 hours of baking time. The pregnant women also had to eat whole cereals, liver, eggs, and fish. Fruit had to be eaten in abundance and green vegetables had to be eaten raw or after a quick cooking.

This diet was then extended to men, women and children—and in a short time the people of Cheshire County enjoyed good health in abundance.

What A Bad Diet Can Do To You

Besides making you old before your time, eating the wrong foods can bring on a slew of ailments you would not ordinarily associate with your eating habits. Yet doctors have learned that the foods that are bad for you can cause:

1. Depressed mood; feeling sad, low, blue hopeless, gloomy.
2. Anhedonia—inability to experience pleasure.
3. Weight loss, poor appetite.
4. Insomnia or hypersomnia.
5. Agitation.
6. Retardation.
7. Loss of energy, fatigue.
8. Decrease in libido.
9. Loss of interest in work and other activities.
10. Feelings of guilt.
11. Diminished ability to think or concentrate.
12. Anxiety or tension.
13. Bodily complaints.

How We're Killing Ourselves

Saint Germain and the other long livers in the world would be horrified if they knew what we do to ourselves. We, too, should be horrified. Our self-abuse is almost criminal. Just think about it for a moment. Recount the ways you are destroying yourself. And in case you don't include all of them, here's a rundown:

Most of us live on a poor diet. We eat too quickly and often on the run. We drink too much coffee, tea and soft drinks. We eat too many sweets, too many carbohydrates, too many foods that do us absolutely no good at all.

Infections wrack us and we don't do anything about them. We find ourselves emotionally disturbed because of stress, jobs, home situations and other causes. We don't allow ourselves enough sleep. We exercise in fits and starts, if at all. We don't walk at all, not even to a corner for a newspaper. We don't bend or stretch. We're tense and we don't know how to combat it. We pop sleeping pills to drop off at night and take amphetamines to pop us up during the day. Include tranquillizers when things don't go right on the job. We sun ourselves to such an extent that we end up with leathery skin and perhaps a case of skin cancer. We drink too much alcohol, smoke too many cigarettes. We work too hard. Our vacations are usually a bust because we don't know how to relax.

The fact that we live as long as we do is a testament to the rugged body that God gave us. It is apparent that if we wish to increase our life-span we must adopt a "New Age Diet," that is radically different from the fast food ritual many of us follow every day. If we're going to live to be as old as the wise men of the Bible, we're going to have to mind our P's and Q's when it comes to eating. Many of those who claim to have experienced contact with advanced extraterrestrial beings coming here in so-called UFOs say they have been told that space beings all live hundreds of years, basically because they know what *not* to put into their systems.

Real Killers—White Bread, White Flour, White Sugar

Before you pooh-pooh the idea that these innocuous foods could be killers, take a look at what's happening in other countries.

Switzerland, for instance, has known about the dangers of white bread for years. In fact, this country tries so hard to discourage its people from eating it that it has placed a tax on it. The tax money goes to the bakers of whole-wheat bread to help bring the price down to the reach of more people.

Canada passed a law prohibiting the enrichment of bread with synthetic vitamins. If a high-vitamin bread appears on the grocery shelves, it must contain the original vitamins found in the wheat, and not imitations.

White bread is actually a "dead" food. This country should be telling us the truth about it and the abomination called "enriched" flour. Before we lay blame on the United States, we must consider the fact that we have really brainwashed ourselves. The government had nothing to do with that.

Our great-great-grandfathers are the real culprits. They started the business of insisting on white bread, white flour and white sugar. In those days, kitchens had to be white. White was synonymous with purity, hence the white bread, sugar and flour. Bakers had no choice but to conform. Those three products now have such a foothold in our diet that they are likely never to be tossed out.

What Does White Bread Contain?

There is a school which says you are better off not knowing. We don't agree. It's important to know what you're eating. With white bread you are eating a bleaching agent which makes the bread white. Bleaches are oxides of nitrogen, chlorine, nitrosyl, chloride, chlorine dioxide, and benzoyl peroxide, mixed with certain chemical salts.

One bleaching ingredient, chloride oxide, combined with whatever proteins are still left in the flour, produces alloxan. This is a poison. It has been used to induce diabetes in laboratory animals.

Chlorine oxide is used to destroy the oil that comes from wheat germ. Bakers don't want that oil in the flour because it makes the flour go sour and nurtures insects.

In the milling process, half the fats are lost. These are the good fats, the unsaturated fatty acids which are high in food value. Vitamin E is lost too in the milling process.

Good quality proteins are removed from the wheat germ and bran. The white flour you buy contains only poor quality proteins.

About 50 percent of all calcium is lost; 70 percent of phosphorus is destroyed; 80 percent of iron is gone; 98 percent of magnesium is lost; 75 percent of manganese, gone; 50 percent of potassium is lost, and 65 percent of copper is destroyed.

Vitamins in white bread and flour also take a beating. Read the losses and weep:

Thiamin—about 80 percent is lost.

Riboflavin—about 60 percent is lost.

Niacin—about 75 percent is lost.

Pantothenic Acid—about 50 percent is lost.

Pyridoxine—about 50 percent is lost.

These figures are the result of a study made by the University of California, College of Agriculture, and the list is not complete here.

Still, it does show us that white bread and white flour do absolutely nothing for us and may even harm us.

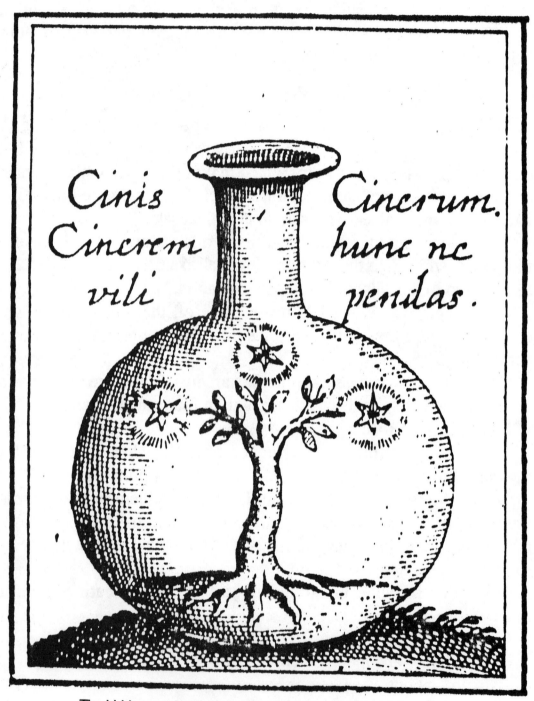

The hidden symbolism of alchemy can be found in historic
pieces of art and literature throughout Europe.

A symbolic drawing of the Tree of Life as seen through the eyes of the alchemist working in his lab with both physical as well as spiritual tools.

Vitamins and Exercise Do You Need Them?

The advice from nutritionists is that if you eat well balanced meals you most certainly get all the vitamins you need. If your doctor prescribes vitamins, then by all means adhere to his advice. The question of vitamins is moot. Some experts feel that a balanced diet is not enough. One is biochemist Robert Benowicz, who says: "We may be getting enough vitamins to prevent vitamin-depletion diseases like scurvy or pellagra, but it's all a matter of the difference between adequate vitamin intake and optimum intake."

The point is, says Benowicz, that each of us is unique, biochemically. A dose of vitamin C may be enough for one person who doesn't smoke, but not enough for another who smokes two packs of cigarettes a day. He says: "The surest way to get every vitamin you want to attempt to reach physical optimum in terms of your body's needs is probably in the form of vitamin supplements. Each of us has got to determine by the variables of our lives what is the optimum vitamin intake for us."

Benowicz urges us to see our own doctors before taking vitamin supplements of any kind, especially if we are taking prescription drugs. He also warns us never to take vitamins when we're sick. "This is folly, go to a doctor."

Exercise for a Long Life

You'll find that most people enjoying longevity participate in some form of exercise. They walk, bend, stretch or move their muscles in other ways. They are physically active. If they have to sit for long periods, they make sure they move about when they can. Doctors say that walking, for instance, can do wonders for the cardiovascular system. They recommend a 15-minute brisk walk every day. A Chicago physician says that if everyone spent an hour a day walking, his waiting room would be less than half full.

The best part about walking is that you don't need any special equipment. You can do it any time of the day and it can be fitted into almost any schedule. And no matter what your age, you can indulge in it to some degree.

Physical therapists tell us that walking can ease tension, cure insomnia, chronic fatigue and plenty of those minor physical ailments that bedevil you. It can also lift your spirits when you're depressed. Psychiatrists say that as long as the body remains in motion the spirits cannot stay low. It's also the perfect remedy for problems of digestion, elimination and circulation. Walking can do a lot more:

1. It strengthens the heart.
2. It deepens and regulates breathing and clears the lungs.
3. It gives the nervous system a healthy boost.
4. Walking strengthens the internal organs as well as muscles.
5. The all-important endocrine glands are activated.
6. Your mental capacities are improved.
7. You will get back more than you give. When walking becomes your daily exercise, you'll find that you will get more energy than you expend.

The first thing you need are comfortable shoes. Your strides should be brisk yet not hurried. Swing your arms freely at your sides and keep your head up. They key is rhythm. Your walk should not be fast-paced, but it should be steady. This is easily accomplished in the country, not at all easy in the city where there are crowds and traffic lights. If you live near a park, use it. Parks are good for walking. Marlene Dietrich always takes long walks in Central Park when she's in New York City. Bing Crosby was a great walker. Actresses Lynn Fontaine and Ingrid Bergman walked every chance they got, and Greta Garbo, now in her 70s, walks everywhere.

One point that must be stressed here is that before you begin any exercise program, check with your doctor first.

Jogging Is a Killer Exercise

This writer has never seen a jogger who looks as though he is enjoying what he's doing. The expression he wears is pained. He looks as though he would rather be doing anything else but running. Actually, he should be doing anything else. If he jogs on city streets he inhales more carbon monoxide then a pack-a-day cigarette smoker. The list of people who have dropped dead or who have been seriously injured by jogging is frighteningly long. On the plus side, it does develop good leg and thigh muscles, accelerates the heart and gives you a chance to breathe fresh air (in the country).

But there are too many negative sides to seriously consider jogging as a method of lengthening your life. Doctors have discovered that jogging can damage the sacroiliac joints, the joints of the spine, the veins of the abdominal rings in men, the uterus and breasts in women.

Jogging can also cause "dropped" stomachs, loosened spleens, floating kidneys and fallen arches. Blood crusts or thrombi on the inner surfaces of the blood vessels may be shaken loose during jogging. If these thrombi are carried to the smaller heart blood vessels they can block them and thereby cause a heart attack.

As we see it, the exercise is a violation of the body. You can get the same results from concentrating on exercises which are far less strenuous. What's more, they won't leave you gasping for breath.

Try a Slant Board for Total Relaxation

It's doubtful if Saint Germain or any of the other long livers used slant boards, but the device can work wonders in your own quest for longevity.

A daily session on a slant board can bring your spine and organs into proper alignment. Blood is forced to the vital areas of the body. The back flattens. Muscles relax. Your feet and legs get a much-needed break from supporting your frame all day. Those same extremities are able, with a slant board, to release congestion into the blood stream and tissues, reducing the possibility of swollen limbs and strained blood vessels.

Your abdominal muscles now have a chance to permit gravity to pull them back into place. When you lie on the board with your head down, blood can flow to your head and firm up your facial muscles. It's also good for the hair and scalp. Experts in Yoga say that the slant board is great for clearing the brain and the brain functions 14 percent better when the head is lower than the feet.

Begin your slant board sessions slowly, building to two 15-minute periods a day. The board is a lot better than trying to stand on your head. Only a few people do it properly and it can be dangerous. You can achieve the same effect with a board, and with no danger.

Other Not-So-Strenuous Exercises

Stretching is a good exercise that won't tax you too much but will get your blood circulating. Try standing on your toes while reaching for the ceiling. Another easy one is to touch the floor without bending your knees. Still another is the chair push-up in which you lean forward with your hands on a chair back. Keep your body straight. Do the push-ups until you feel tired. This is easier than doing push-ups on the floor.

If you do those exercises for a total of about six minutes a day you'll see a big difference in your physical and mental well-being. However, it's always a good idea to check with your doctor before you start any kind of exercise program. It's also best not to start the program if you are more than 40 pounds overweight. Reduce first, then exercise.

You Can't Flirt With Exercise

That's the catch. Once you start an exercise program you have to stick with it. Make it part of your daily routine. Find out for yourself which part of the day is best for you to devote to the exercises. If you bounce out of bed in the morning, that may be the best time for you. If you peak at mid-morning, then do the exercises then.

After a week you won't feel any better. Don't let that concern you. It does take a lot of time before you see changes. What you must not do is to try to hurry the process with more strenuous work-outs. That's a no-no. It's risky. Besides, you'll take the fun out of it.

What Should Oldsters Do About Exercise?

In 1970, the West Virginia Commission on Aging assigned physical therapist Lawrence J. Frankel to develop a physical fitness program for the elderly. The choice was a wise one. Frankel had already had experience designing an exercise program for asthmatic children in the mid-1950s. He'd also worked out a gymnastic program for blind children.

Frankel studied the problem of designing a program for the elderly and told the Commission:

Older people do not exercise because they have been stereotyped as senior citizens, and society says that they should not exercise. As a result, many withdraw from physical activities and become more and more immobile, which ultimately can lead to institutionalization. We've got to motivate elderly people to be more active if they are to resist the ravages nd the unhappiness of old age.

With the help of a collaborator, physical fitness expert Mrs. Betty Richard, Frankel set up a series of 50 simple exercises. They were tested in Charleston on 15 people aged 60 to 86. The results were astounding.

Using his program called Preventicare, one 75-year-old woman saw her life turned around completely. She had been bedridden. She lived in an apartment residence peopled by oldsters. One of the requirements was that she be ambulatory and that she be capable of caring for herself. She could not. Her next step was a nursing home.

After doing the Preventicare exercises for a short time, she was able to get out of bed, walk, cook her own meals and do other chores. She was able to attend social classes and affairs and even lead a group in exercises. Her notice of eviction was cancelled.

The test on the 15 people was so successful that Frankel was asked to establish Preventicare programs in other housing projects for the elderly, old folks' homes and hospitals. Today there are about 200 Preventicare groups in 51 of the 55 counties in West Virginia. Groups can also be found in New York, Virginia, Kentucky, Ohio, Pennsylvania and North Dakota.

Groups run from 10 to 30 people, and their ages range from 60 to 102. The only requirement to join a group is a doctor's certificate stating that the applicant is able to perform the exercises.

The equipment is inexpensive. A strip of carpet is needed, or padding to sit on, a medicine ball and a length of broomstick for certain exercises. No outside instructors are needed. Each group selects its own leader from the group. Each session lasts one hour. There is no fee. Expenses are minimal. There are no physical strains. The exercises are done to soft background music. The idea is to keep the pulse rate below 120 beats per minute, which is considered the highest rate elderly people can safely attain. There are at least three sessions a week.

Frankel says:

After people reach their 60s, most begin to suffer from poor circulation, aching joins and muscles, and bone degeneration. Their coordination declines, and they experience chronic fatigue. However, with the right exercises, elderly people can improve their circulation, fortify their hearts and lungs, tone up their muscles. Most of them can get back their mobility.

Monsieur

Connoissant depuis longtems votre Gout pour les livres rares, & le Soin que vous prenez d'en enrichir continuellement votre belle & nombreuse Bibliotheque, j'ai cru que je vous ferois plaisir de vous parler d'une des plus rares & des plus singulieres qu'on connoisse; puisque c'est un Exemplaire de la seconde de toutes les Editions du Monde faites avec des Caracteres mobiles. La premiere, comme vous le savez sans doute, est une Bible Latine, dont Trithême parle sous l'Année 1450 de ses Annales Hirsaugienses, et après lui Mrs Chevillier, Maittaire, & quantité d'autres. La seconde, qui est celle dont il s'agit, & que je puis vous procurer, est un Catholicon Joannis Januensis, inconnu à tous les Bibliothecaires, excepté les seuls Peres Quetif & Echard, qui en parlent ainsi dans leurs Scriptores Ordinis Predicatorum recensiti, Tom. I, pag. 462, ce que vous pouvez vérifier. Altera (la premiere étoit une Edition en Planches de Bois du même Livre, qui fut le 1er Ouvrage réel de Guttemberg, Fust, & Schoiffer, et auquel succeda la Bible Latine en Caracteres mobiles:) altera ex Arte Typographica a° 1450 tum perfectâ, tamen absque Numeris, Signaturis, Reclamationibus, Anno, Loco, Nomine Typothetae; absque Litteris etiam initialibus, quae omnes [illegible] et pictae: quam Moguntiae prodisse conjiciunt. Extat ejusce Exemplaar Parisiis, in Genovefinâ Bibliothecâ, in folio maximo Chartâ Regiâ.

L'Exemplaire que j'ai est tout semblable à celui-là; et il n'y a nul Doute, qu'il ne sort de Mayence, et de l'Imprimerie des trois premiers Imprimeurs de cette Ville & du Monde, puisque le Papier sur lequel il est imprimé porte les Mêmes Marques que celui sur lequel Schoiffer seul imprima son Decretum Gratiani en 1472. Le Caractere est tout semblable pour la Forme, mais un peu plus petit, que celui de la Bible Latine de 1462, et ses Pages sont beaucoup plus hautes et plus larges, chaque colonne aiant 65 lignes au lieu que celles de la Bible n'en ont que quarante-huit. Que ce Catholicon soit plus ancien que

Quant à l'Exemplaire que j'ai, il est parfaitement bien conservé, et relié en Bois couvert de Peau de Truie, semée de Fleurs de Lis, cantonnées chacune de quatre Rosaces, et renfermées dans des Lozanges formées par de triples Lignes se croisant les unes les autres de Biais, de toute la Hauteur du Volume, et renfermées elles-mêmes dans un Cadre ou Bordure de Dragons, divisés par une longue Bande courant en Zig-Zag; &, sur cette Couverture, il y avoit autrefois des Cous & des Bossettes, dont les Marques se distinguent très bien encore. Il est de plus antiqué sur la Tranche, et lavé et reglé, non seulement à l'ordinaire autour de chaque Page, mais extraordinairement sous chaque Ligne: &, outre que les grandes Lettres qui commencent chacun des Traittés et Chapitres sont enrichies de Fleurons & Feuillages peints en Vermillon et en Azur, toutes celles du commencement de chaque Article du Dictionaire, ce qui va à un Nombre infini, sont des mêmes Couleurs alternativement, depuis le Commencement jusqu'à la fin. Ce sont deux Tomes in folio, qui font un Volume d'une Grandeur & Grosseur extraordinaire. On n'y voit rien d'écrit à la main, come dans la plûpart des vieux Livres, qui en sont fort défigurez.

Tel est, Monsieur, le Livre, dont j'ai cru devoir me donner l'Honneur de vous écrire, & dont je ne me serois point avisé de vous importuner, si ce n'etoit une Piéce extraordinaire, très rare*, & tout-à-fait digne d'occuper une Place dans une Bibliotheque aussi célèbre & aussi renommée que la Vôtre. Afin que Vous puissiez la faire examiner par quelque Personne de Confiance ici, je prendrai la liberté de joindre à tout ceci mon Adresse, après vous avoir assuré très humblement du Respect avec lequel je suis,

* Elle ne se trouve nulle part ailleurs qu'à Ste Genevieve de Paris

Monsieur,

A la Haye, ce 22. Novbre 1735.

Votre très humble & très obeissant Serviteur
P. M. de St Germain chez la Veuve Vincent, sur le Nieuwe-Haven, in de Tuyn-Laan.

Proof that Saint Germain lived in the seventeenth century can be found in the British Museum in the form of a letter written in French by the Count.

Too Much Stress Can Kill?

We are built physically and mentally to handle stress. Without some stress in our lives our bodies and minds would deteriorate. You experience physical stress when you work too hard at tasks that require your muscle power. If you exercise too much you are under physical stress. If you are injured, or contract a disease, you are in a physically stressful situation.

Our minds thrive on stress. But not too much of it. We need to have mental stimulation. If we don't get it we stagnate. If our minds are deprived of stimulation or occupation for any length of time, the situation becomes intolerable. And that in itself is a form of stress.

We are under more stress than you would imagine. It comes to us at home, on the job, in public transportation, on the street, and in shops. We are under stress when we try to pass a slow driver on the road, when we shop for an item we can't find, when we have to endure the noise of a subway, a machine shop, a loud-playing radio, a traffic jam. Our stress and annoyance increase when we try to talk above the din.

The Dangers of Psychological Stress

Dr. Aaron T. Beck, professor of psychiatry at the University of Pennsylvania, tells us that in his psychiatric practice he sees two major types of stress. One involves the loss of a loved one, or a job, or of self-esteem. The other involves threats to the individual's status, goals, health or security. Dr. Beck says: "Such stresses can generate symptoms of depression or anxiety of both. And today, statistics indicate that severe depression or anxiety may involve 20 percent of Americans at one point or another in their lives."

Stress During Life Changes

Dr. Thomas Holmes, professor of psychiatry at the University of

Washington, devised a stress scale which assigns a point value to changes, good or bad, that can affect us. He found in the population he studied that when enough changes occur during one year to add up to 300, a danger point has been reached. According to his research, 80 percent of the people who exceeded 300 became seriously depressed, had heart attacks or suffered other serious illnesses.

Listed below are the life changes and the points assigned to them:

Life Changes	Points
Death of Spouse	100
Divorce	73
Marital separation	65
Jail term	63
Death of close family member	63
Personal injury or illness	53
Marriage	50
Fired from job	47
Marital reconciliation	45
Retirement	45
Change in health of family member	44
Pregnancy	40
Sex difficulties	39
Gain of new family member	39
Change in financial status	38
Death of close friend	37
Change to different kind of work	36
Change in number of arguments with spouse	35
Foreclosure of a mortgage or a loan	30
Change in work responsibilities	29
Son or daughter leaving home	29
Trouble with in-laws	29
Outstanding personal achievement	28
Wife beginning or stopping work	26
Beginning or ending school	26
Revision of personal habits	24
Trouble with boss	23
Change in residence	20
Change in schools	20
Vacation	13
Minor violations of the law	11

Making Stress Work For You

The late Dr. Hans Selye, a Nobel laureate and president of the International Institute of Stress in Montreal, Canada, was a leading expert on stress. He was a master at using his energy where it counted. He said, "I never try to avoid stress because it is an inescapable part of life. I just try to make it work for me and give me pleasure instead of pain. I feel each person is his own best doctor and must determine his own stress level."

Dr. Selye was in his late 70s when he died. He had two artificial hips and hobbled when he walked. He also had reticulosarcoma, one of the most malignant cancers known to mankind. The disease is fatal in 99.5 percent of the cases. Dr. Selye accepted the disease as one of the greatest challenges of his life. He refused to give up. He saw years pass before he finally succumbed to it. He said at one point: "There have been some very interesting studies. Sloan Kettering Institute among others found that when people truly want to live, they make a greater effort and their immunization system somehow works better."

Dr. Selye's pet theory was that stress might be the cause of disease. He said that when the body is under stress for a long period of time, it reacts in a certain way. He called the reaction G.A.S. (general adaption syndrome). He described G.A.S. as coming in three stages.

1. The alarm reactor when the body stirs its defense mechanism—the glands, hormones, and nervous system—into action.

2. The adaptation stage when the body fights back.

3. The stage of exhaustion, when the body's defenses can no longer cope. This eventually leads to death.

Dr. Selye said that stress is the rate of all of the wear and tear on our bodies caused by life. "It is the body's response to any demand. But without making demands on any of our capacities we would all be dead. Our goal should be to live in the manner that gives us the most pleasure and the least distress." The expert added that there is a mountain of evidence to indicate that great joy produces the same nonspecific biochemical changes in the body as intense pain. It doesn't make any difference whether the agent is pleasure or pain. The only thing that counts is the intensity of the demand for readjustment or adaptation.

Dr. Selye said that surprisingly, rest does not relieve exposure to great stress. Animal experiments have demonstrated that such exposure to stress leaves an indelible scar and that it uses up an adaptability reserve that can't be replaced.

The expert said:

> The crucial thing is not so much what happens to you, but the way you react to it.
>
> Blocking the fulfilment of our natural drives to a great degree for any length of time can be a very dangerous thing.
>
> If you do what you like, you really never work. Your work is your play.
>
> All I'm telling people is to do their own thing.
>
> I just don't think that much about age. I'm aware as I become older that I have less energy for simply physical reasons. I can't run as fast as I used to. But it isn't so bad, because even if my capacity to do things has somewhat diminished, the quality of enjoyment is still there. The most important thing is not just to add years to life, but to add life to the years.

Stress—A Tough Hurdle for Oldsters

Younger people can usually handle stress better than the elderly because they have more physical resilience and reserves. They have not yet been scarred too deeply by life. Dr. Ruth B. Weg, a physiologist at the University of Southern California's Andrus Gerontology Center, says that the aged have a diminished ability to respond to stress and that as we grow older stress causes greater physiological displacement and recovery from it takes longer. There is evidence that a high-stress lifestyle appears to accelerate the aging process. Still, there are many oldsters whose lives have been stress-filled, yet they do go on living to advanced ages.

Dr. Weg says:

> Admittedly, there are decrements in physiological function with time. Yet these changes are gradual and there is more than enough capacity left to independent living. The data demonstrate that to the extent that people use, nourish, and extend the remaining capacities, body and spirit will benefit and the whole person will prosper.

She suggests that, like people of other ages, older folks should take positive preventive action to strengthen themselves against the ill effects of too much stress.

The Concept of Fight or Flight

When a cave man was faced with a ferocious animal, he knew nothing about the body changes taking place within him. When cornered, his brain programmed him into a fight or flight response. No matter which he decided to do, his body was prepared for peak performance. His involuntary nervous system switched on secretions of adrenalin and other hormones. His blood pressure rose. His heart beat faster. There was a sharp rise in his breathing and metabolism. He was ready to fight...or run.

Psychiatrists say that we still need this means of self-preservation on occasion, although the idea is not to respond to the emotional traumas and anxieties of modern living. This is where danger lies. The repeated overworking of the heart and the upsurge in blood pressure increases the likelihood of chronic hypertension.

In short, we must avoid stress whenever we can.

How to Cope with Stress

Living simply can eliminate lots of stress. Examine your problems intelligently rather than emotionally. Talking to a friend is a great way to alleviate stress. Dr. Ira Altshuler of Detroit says that too many men die prematurely because they never talked out their anxieties. Their wives lasted much longer because they chatted on the phone or across the back fence. If they didn't talk so much their blood pressures would soar.

Meditation is another way to relieve stress. It's not really hard to do. Dr. Herbert Benson of Harvard says that meditation is an easy, effective relaxation technique—and relaxation is the physiological opposite of stress.

In his book, *The Relaxation Response,* Dr. Benson says that meditation brings about a marked decrease in heart rate, breathing, muscle tension and other factors associated with stress. He describes a simple procedure to relieve stress.

1. Sit in a comfortable position, quietly, with your eyes closed.

2. Relax your muscles deeply. Start at your feet and work your way up to your face. Keep them relaxed.

3. Breathe easily and naturally through your nose. Every time you exhale, say a word. You might use the word "one," or any simple word of your own choosing. But say it silently to yourself.

4. Do it for ten or 20 minutes with eyes closed. You'll have to open them to check the time, but don't use an alarm clock.

5. Sit for several minutes with your eyes closed after you have fin-

ished. Open them and sit still for another few minutes.

6. You are not likely to achieve deep relaxation at your first attempt. But it will come. Let it come at its own place. If you are distracted by disturbing thoughts, try to ignore them by repeating your favorite word over and over again. Practice the technique once or twice a day and you'll soon learn the pleasure of deep relaxation.

There are some "ifs" involved here. Dr. Benson said that if you have hypertension, you should see your doctor about it first. If you practice too soon after eating, the digestive process will interfere. Wait two hours after eating. If you intend to use meditation as a substitute for medical treatment, don't.

Other Stress Relievers

According to the experts, such things as mini-vacations can do wonders for the stress-filled individual. And that includes even a few minutes during the day. Dr. Sara M. Jordan said: "It is wonderful to see how the greatest stress can be endured by the human body if periods of relaxation are interspersed at enough intervals."

How You Can Live Forever

Count Saint-Germain did it with his mysterious elixirs; we can do it with the best advice from gerontologists who have studied the problems of longevity for years.

Overall, Americans are not long livers. In the world, we rank 24th for men and ninth for women. American men live an average of 67.1 years and American women 74.6 years. We don't do as well as people in Western Europe, Japan, Israel, Greece, East Germany and Australia. We also rank behind people in the Netherlands, Sweden, Iceland, Norway, Denmark, France, Canada and Great Britain.

The only thing we can boast about when it comes to longevity is that we are doing better than our ancestors, who suffered pestilence and famine, and who had to witness the horribly high rate of infant deaths and maternity deaths.

In ancient Rome the average lifespan was 22 years. In Western Europe during the Middle Ages the average rose to 33 years. In 1900 everywhere, life expectancy was 47 years.

That was the turning point. Between 1900 and 1950, something dramatic happened. The average lifespan leaped 20 years. One of the factors was medicine's successes in wiping out child-killer diseases. Another was that people were learning how to take care of themselves. During those five decades, diets improved, new emphasis was placed on vitamins and nutrition, better medical facilities, shorter work weeks and longer leisure periods in which to pursue other interests and a great involvement in exercise programs.

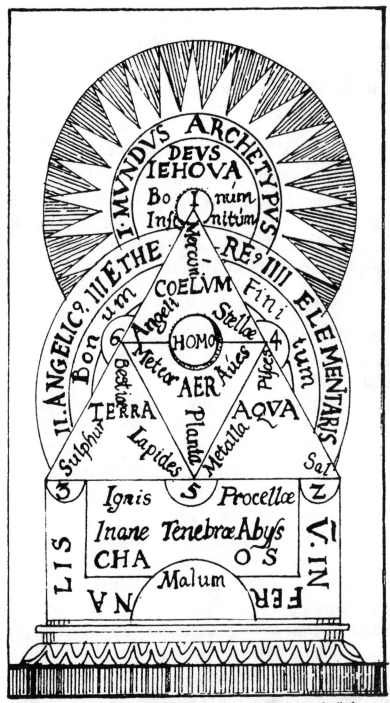

As above, so below best describes the alchemists belief
in the magickal workings of the universe

An alchemist speaks to one of the invisible Masters who appears before him to give him advice in his work.

Secrets of Longevity

The experts say we can live longer if we have a sense of purpose and direction, if we have a feeling of belonging, and if we are loved.

It's no coincidence that married people everywhere live longer than those who are single, divorced and widowed. Britain's coronary thrombosis rate is 40 percent higher among widowers than among married men of the same age.

A sense of belonging was really misunderstood until World War II, when the British had to rally against a common enemy. At that time, the death rate from suicide and alcohol in that country dropped to nearly zero.

Living Long is Up to Us, Individually

There is no such unity in the United States. Few nations in the world today are rallied against a common enemy. So living a long time is now a personal goal. We have an obligation to ourselves to live long. Our government does help by trying to eliminate poverty, disease, and by educating us on the dangers of overindulgence. But in the end, the problem is ours. We can't go the route of Count Saint-Germain because apparently he did everything that was bad for us, yet survived perhaps five generations. But we can be sensible and serious about keeping ourselves alive for as long as possible, and not simply alive but alive and productive.

The Secrets to Insure Longevity

Roger J. Samp of the University of Wisconsin studied 1,000 persons who were 75 and older. He learned that these people did not take part in any rigid exercise program, but did walk a lot and were mentally active. All, without exception, enjoyed being with other people. Most still enjoyed sex. None overate and there were no alcoholic binges. Most slept well, getting about eight hours of sleep a night. There were few cigarette smokers and no heavy smokers.

One important point Samp learned concerned stress. Almost every one of the old people told him that they had always avoided stress on their jobs. If they did not enjoy their work, they quit and found other jobs.

Most had hobbies. Some kept three or four going at the same time.

Finally, they all enjoyed a good laugh.

Dr. Edward L. Bortz of Philadelphia is a member of the American Medical Association Committee on Aging. He has composed a checklist on how to live longer and better. We offer the list here:

1. A balanced diet including more protein, vitamins, and fluids; fewer fats and calories.

2. Regular elimination of waste products.

3. Adequate rest of both mind and body.

4. Pursuit of interesting and specific recreational activities.

5. A sense of humor.

6. Avoidance of excessive emotional tension that leads to personal ineffectiveness.

7. Mutual loyalty of friends and family.

8. Pride in a job.

9. Participation in community affairs.

10. Continued expansion of knowledge, wisdom, and experience.

Socialize and Live Longer

Whether you think so or not, we do thrive when we are with people. You need people and people need you. A study by Lisa Berkman, a California epidemiologist, discovered that people with many good friends, strong family ties and membership in social or religious groups apparently have a better chance of living longer than lonely people. The study was based on 7,000 residents of Alameda County, California. It found that almost any form of social tie was associated with longevity. The study also showed that unmarried folks who had many friends and relatives had about the same mortality rate as married people with few friends and relatives. Both were better off than single, lonely people.

Only by experiencing participation in a community project can you really understand the pleasure you get from it. Unfortunately, however, too many of us are willing to sit back and say, "Let George do it." We pop down in front of our TV screens and become willing spectators. We're bored. But we don't know what else to do. We're willing to wait for something to happen to us rather than be the driving force to make something happen. Boredom, says one psychiatrist, is an illness…and one that can kill us if we're not careful.

We Need to Laugh More

Communing with others just about insures good laughs. The Illinois State Medical Society says laugh and be healthy. Dr. Sara M. Jordan of the Lahey Clinic in Boston says laugh and live long.

Laughing is a group emotion. It breaks the strain of an emotional upset, snaps tensions and gives your glands a boost so that they can do their work. It's a respiratory exercise which is wonderful for your chest organs. And when we say laughter we don't mean a smirk, a smile, a grin or a chuckle; we mean a deep, loud type of laugh that folks of the old days would call a "knee-slapping roar."

For a Long Life,
Don't Forget the Power of Prayer

Prayer works. We don't know how or why, but it does. It's hard to believe that the subject has never been fully explored. Non one has really researched it. Charles Steinmetz, the electrical genius of General Electric Company, said that the next realm of research would be spiritual, and the next field of study would be prayer. His prediction has not yet come true.

Dr. Norman Vincent Peal says: "Prayer is the greatest power in the world. It is a pity more people do not know how to use it."

One question that always arises is: How does one pray? Do we rattle off words by rote? Or is it a series of loving thoughts directed at the thing we want. It is neither. What we have to do first is relax. Then accept the fact that there is a power without trying to analyze whether it comes from above or is merely autosuggestion. No matter where the power comes from, it is there for the asking. So ask for it.

The next step is to direct the power to what you want done. In this case it would be longevity. In your mind's eye, visualize yourself in your golden years, active, happy and productive. You see yourself as a healthy human being. What you are doing in effect is seeing your prayers answered.

When you are finished praying, give thanks that what you want accomplished will be done. When you've done that, you have prayed effectively and correctly.

Lonely People Die Young

You don't have to put up with loneliness. We can make sure we have a circle of friends at all times. Dr. John W. McKelvey said: "I am convinced that loneliness is 90 percent self-pity. The victim shuts himself in, others out. Everybody avoids him, for nobody loves a self-pitier."

What we can do about it first is to stop being self-centered. Look for new interests. Look for ways to help others. If we do those things we will find that our loneliness has vanished.

To Live Long, Be Mature

One test of maturity is to know where you are important, and where you are not important. The mature individual knows he is different from everyone else in the world. He is unique. He has no desire to be like someone else. He wants to be himself. He wants to be important to himself, his family, his friends and his community. He loves, and is loved.

Inner peace is achieved by growing up. If we have immaturities left over from childhood, we must deal with them. They can't be hidden. We can't assume that they will go away. We must consciously seek maturity by making a positive adjustment to living which comes from knowing ourselves.

All of which boils down to the fact that we must not be afraid to be ourselves, being different. The world is not in need of blind conformists. It needs more people who are unique, who are different, and who can capitalize on their uniqueness.

What is maturity? Dr. Norman Vincent Peale says that the mature person never admits that his situation or position is catastrophic. He does not borrow trouble. He does not panic or allow himself to be engulfed by imaginary fears. He does not over-dramatize a situation or waste time with regrets.

The French philosopher Henri Bergson says: "To exist is to change, to change is to mature, to mature is to go on creating oneself endlessly."

Psychic impressionist artist, Carol Ann Rodriguez, senses that Saint Germain is still very active as an alchemist performing his rituals to this day in an underground monastery beneath the mountains surrounding Tibet.

Saint Germain in the New Age

In an issue of the metaphysical magazine, *Search*, mystic writer Alfred Taber gives a good overview of Saint Germain's purpose in relation to current New Age teachings which more-or-less cements our own understanding of his work as we close in on the turn of the century.

• • •

There are today in existence and steadily growing in numbers many new religions dedicated to a New-Age, particularly one headed by the already well known Master Personages who instituted the Theosophist movement in the last century.

Prophets and seers are not the special property of a particular age or country but have appeared from time to time especially when the world was undergoing crucial changes, today is such a time, perhaps the very most important one of them all. Where there is a flock, there must be a Shepherd; whenever the earth needs special assistance the Shepherd must appear. These Shepherds have announced that the dawning of a New Age—a Permanent Golden Age—is upon us, that we are already within it. This Age is being presided over and headed by the Master Saint Germain.

The transition problems into this New Age will be quite difficult because of every person. But inasmuch as this crossing of the "Red Sea" will be difficult, the reward will be very great, resulting in an Era of Freedom.

We can see that the years of the twentieth century are drawing to a close which means the ending of an important preparatory circle but not at all as important as the one ahead.

The formation of this new religion was brought about by three impulses or movements starting with very successful Theosophism, which was under the direction of a personage known to many as the Master Kuthumi. The next action was brought about by his well known Master —Brother El Morya who is still very active. Now we are in the third and final phase under the direction of the Maha Chohan.

Some may ask what is meant by the statement that an Age of Freedom is at hand, since such ones feel that they are already free, especially in the United States. People cannot know what true freedom really is until they have experienced it. There can be no real freedom until people can control causes. Until now most people have been the prey of internal and external causes of distress due to their accidental and unillumined use of life. This haphazard and often wrong use will be remedied by the intervention of a new agent. The New Age is termed Permanent because of many new provisions and safeguards among which is one of the most important—the expanded Christ—Agent within each heart. This, of course, is the "Second Coming," how else can an age be permanent unless this transmuting and directive mentor be brought to bear and guide each personality?

In the last few years, especially, mankind has been within the crucible of purification where a constant cleansing activity has been brought to play upon them by an action destined to be very much before the popular mind—The Violet-Fire.

The age ahead will be one incorporating to a large degree this Violet Fire of freedom from the beloved Saint Germain. As this is brought more and more into action the violet-coloration will be seen about us to a larger degree. We can see it already in a much freer use of this color which was very rarely incorporated in such things as automobiles, umbrellas, clothing, songs and other things.

The New Age Religion will be one of ordered service dealing with, among other things, ceremonial activities in which, it is promised, the Angelic and Elemental Kingdoms will be combined in mankind's worship. This will be a state where mankind will be cognizant of the Angelic Kingdom and we can well assert that many of the so-called "saucers" seen in the sky are none other than these, already faintly visible. In the coming age the organization known as the Great White Brotherhood is to gently incorporate into itself the rest of mankind bringing about true unity, true love, true brotherhood. Speaking of brotherhood it is well to note that the new religion and age has had its fitting inception in the city of Brotherly Love, where stands that other great symbol of freedom: Independence Hall with its "Liberty" Bell.

In past ages and religions nontheism and polytheism were integrated into different eras resulting usually in a golden age, but unfortunately as soon as the seed of decay "took root" and the people left their gods the moral fibre crumbled resulting in degradation. Before the new impulse reaches sufficient strength, America, its beacon, will probably have to cope with degradation but help is directed here, as for instance in having other problem nations as an impetus to keep this country going ahead and not leisurely falling asleep.

The Jewish religion is a monotheistic one as is to a large extent the Christian. The Age of St. Germain is, in the main, polytheistic, but monotheistic in a sense; unifying all of the past saviors and goddesses into a combined whole so that no person will be required to give up an affinity to any such being.

With each new cycle it is required of nature to provide adequately for the evolving humanity with necessary spiritual food, for this is an integral part of existence, and is shown in the symbol of the interlaced triangles where both are interdependent; the ascending prayer force from mankind with the resultant response from the Upper Octaves in a descending triangle to equalize the demand, where the law is that the call must be answered, whether collective or singular.

The religion is based on direct revelation and guidance as to its formation and development from the masters and much of the instruction constitutes their very own words, resulting in a clarification of the Bible.

Mankind is becoming increasingly more tolerant of new forms of worship as a need is being felt to supplement the old with the new.

The test of a new religion is in the products of its members, especially its leaders, and can only become a major one if it can produce major works, for example is all-important. Miraculous and wonderful things are already associated with this impulse and much dealing with heretofore secret information, accessible only to vowed inmates, has lavishly been given out. These are an extension as well as a clarification of age-old principles.

The religion aims to refine and purify the member by giving from its body, vitality, and nourishment culminating, through gentle service on the part of the devotee, in the Ascension.

The Ascension is possible only when individuals have equalized their debt to life and give of their gift which each has developed through the centuries, and when one is capable of generating a reasonable amount of Impersonal Love, then is it possible to pass from the constant repetition of the life-cycle where the greater beauty of the inner spheres may be enjoyed.

As in the past, women will be of prime importance in rooting this already large impetus into each household. They have a natural tendency to be concerned with personalities and the large array of Divine Beings to be presented will be of natural interest to them.

As will be gathered from the above, among the major precepts of this new way, is instruction concerning certain already well known ideas regarding reincarnation. The public already has a fresh dose of this in having books like "Bridey Murphy" etc., presented before its consciousness.

Belief will now be supplemented with true faith; with knowledge. Dogma may not bring about the necessary transformation unless it is accompanied with personal experience and development which in the case of some present disciples is quite extraordinary verging on sainthood.

The new Religion and Age is to bring about the lowering of the Kingdom of Heaven upon the earth in the form of exquisite architecture (which beginning can already be seen); numerous temples dedicated to the different etheric flames—which will be visible by then, and the many facets of perfection such as clothing the earth in a garden and, of course, the most beautiful part will be the externalization of the Christ within each heart.

The Seventh Age, as pointed out, will be directed by Saint Germain; "the Wonder Man of Europe" (not to be confused with an imposter who used his name). It has been his dream of forming the United States of Europe, which finally culminated in the United States of America. This very great Being (the positive pole of the Violet Fire) also has the assistance of the Goddess Kwan Yin known as the "Mother of Mercy."

For those who already feel the faint promptings of their hearts, for those who can overlook the discontent of the body in giving up the old, it is suggested that true happiness now as in the past, cannot be had while disregarding the expanding tricolored flame in the heart (blue, yellow & rose). This Flame will not be denied for it is being fed from the outside.

Those who will cooperate quickly with it will increase while those who won't will decrease.

America is the beacon which is to light the torch of each brother-nation. Nature has come to us and will not leave until it gives of itself the New Age, adding to its already evident gifts of political, economic and other freedoms, Eternal Freedom, so that each one of us (emulating that great goddess Liberty) can hold high our torches so that all can see...the New Age.

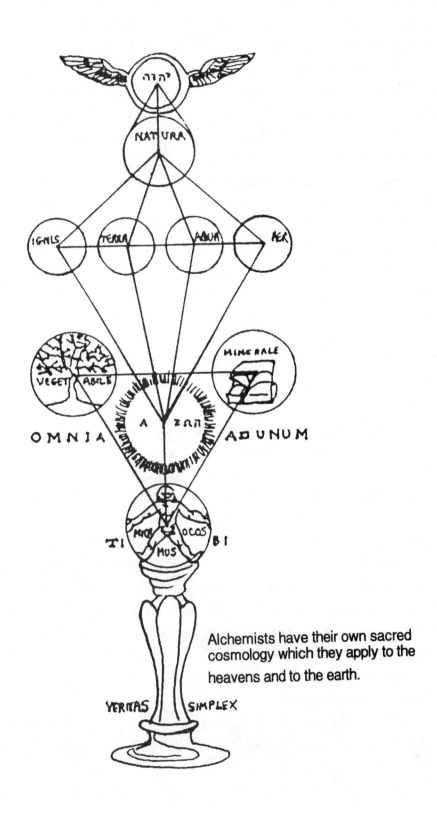

Alchemists have their own sacred cosmology which they apply to the heavens and to the earth.

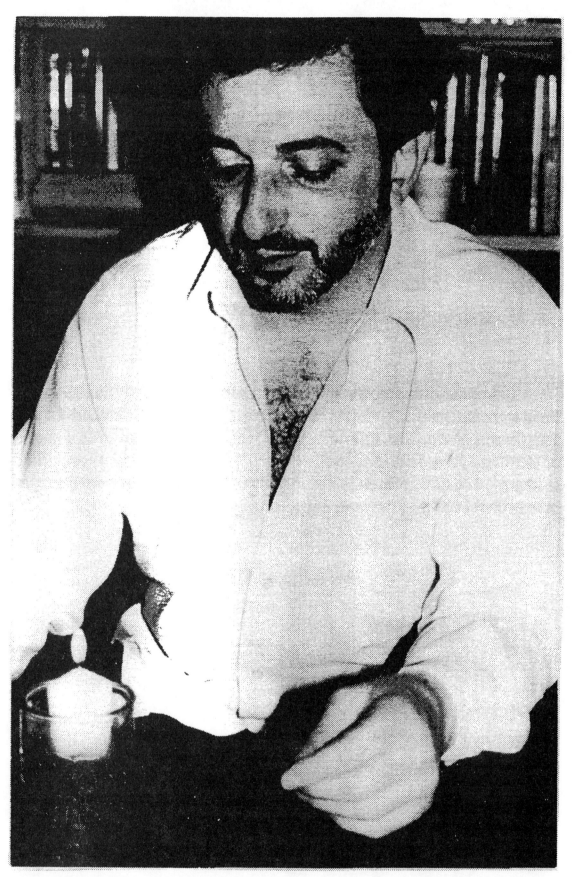

Master metaphysician William Alexander Oribello—seen here doing a blessing with a burning candle—says he first met St. Germain as a boy living in Philadelphia. Today, he channels messages from the New Age prophet who lives forever.

Channeled Messages From Saint Germain

Received through the Master Teacher,
William Alexander Olibello

It is commonly known by seekers everywhere, that Count St. Germain transmits and channels messages through several different mediums around the world. The following messages were received over a period of time, and have not been published until now. At this time I would like to share these messages with the readers of this book. They are arranged in numerical order as they were received.

#1. On Making Right Choices

All disciples of the Path are aware of the Law of Compensation, that "as a man sows, so shall he reap." Therefore, they try to do whatever is necessary to have a good relationship with others, at entry level of human transaction. But there are times when the seeker will do what is right and still offend others. This causes much grief for those who really want to do what is right. Every person must learn to think things through and respect the choices of others. Therefore, always to do what is right, make your choice, and realize that others may not agree with you. They may even accuse you of wrongdoing, but if your intentions were true, then be at peace with your choice.

#2. Love

To some people, love is having those you care about always near at hand, and for as long as those they care about conduct their lives according to someone's wishes. But when a person must choose another path, those who say they love such a person may (and often do) turn against them, in one way or another. Such is imperfect love. Stop and ask your-self why you love, or do not love, this person or that one. Perfect love releases all who concern our lives, in full consideration for their views and decisions. Love lets go, in peace, realizing that every person must grow in their own way. Love gives, without hoping or demanding for anything in return.

#3. Positive Thinking

It is necessary for one on the Path to think positively, in order that they may come to a degree of contentment in their physical existence. This is why personal success is so important: if one determines his or her talent, and develops that talent, so that they achieve some degree of success, then that person will have the leisure to pursue high contemplations. Do not dwell on defeat or past mistakes. Exist within the moment. Generate a feeling of health, wealth and happiness, regardless of your present circumstances. Think happiness in all you say and do, as though all of your fondest dreams become your daily reality.

#4. Forgiveness

When asked for instruction on how to pray, Master Jesus revealed his famous Lord's Prayer, replete with esoteric activators. One part of this prayer deals with forgiveness: "and forgive us our trespasses, as we forgive those who trespass against us." There is healing power in these words, a power that will heal the deepest emotional and mental wounds. As we spend quality time alone in the silence of contemplation, let us try to understand ourselves, how that we have made mistakes but are going through the process of growing. Let us try to understand others, and realize that they are also growing and becoming in their own way. Forgive others, and you will be able to forgive yourself.

#5. Faith

There are those who doubt even the smallest of miracles: they witness the miracle of birth, life and intelligence; the changing of the seasons; the rising and setting of the sun, and the precision by which other planetary bodies follow their course. Are these small miracles? They are small in the sense that we take them for granted. But in reality, these, and several others, are great miracles that happen every day. Yet there are those who experience but do not understand. The same power that moves the mighty forces of nature is the same power that is part of your individual life. If you can adjust your attitude to accept this possibility, then you can work miracles of health, wealth and happiness in your everyday life. Believe in yourself. Not in the self who has failed and feels inferior, but the true-self who is really you, and who is able to work miracles. Do not try too hard to have faith—simply believe in yourself and the Godpower within you.

This is the alchemist symbol for the Fountain of Youth embracing the sacred mysteries of the sun, moon, serpent as well as all the elements of nature.

Meditations & Contemplated Symbols, Channeled by Count Saint Germain

The following meditations and symbols were channeled by Count St. Germain, for the purpose of assisting the student in his/her quest to perfect the five important keys of mastery, and expressed in the five channeled messages within this book.

To use these meditations, just follow these simple instructions: first make sure that you do this when you are alone and will not be disturbed. Take the phone off the hook and dim the lights, except enough light to read by. Second, sit in a comfortable chair, holding this book in your hands. Third, close your eyes and breathe deeply for several moments. Then breathe normally, but focus your attention on your breathing for several minutes. This will help to relax you completely so that you may enter the Inner Temple of Silence. Fourth, when you feel that the time is right, gaze at the first symbol for several moments until you feel a subtle spiritual energy within your being. Then read the first meditation. If you can, read it out loud in a soft but firm voice. After reading the first medication, fix your attention back to the first symbol for several moments. Then close your eyes and relax for a few moments, after which you will look at the second symbol and read the second meditation. Repeat this practice with all five symbols and meditations.

These instructions may be followed whenever you desire. The more often you practice, the better results you will obtain. When you are finished with your meditations, get up and go about your daily business. Do not think about your meditations too much in between sessions—release your desires to the cosmos. However, you should try to be alert to events which present themselves in your life's experience, bringing you closer to your goals.

The figure of Mercury stands as the symbol of eternal
youth in the practice of alchemy.

Meditation #1.

I affirm that I desire to make the right choices at all levels of my life. Therefore, I will keep clear mental images of what I wish to be and what I wish to accomplish. I am that I am: all that my heart desires shall be in harmony with my ultimate good. I resonate to the Universal Mind–God and Goddess. I resonate to perfection in all forms, and by doing so shall make the right choices for my success.

I will no longer worry about what others think of me, so long as I follow my own path with a clean heart and a clear conscience. I realize that I must let go of the painful past. There were people with whom it was necessary to part. There were situations best left behind, and I cannot go back.

I begin from this moment to reach out—not for what has been—but for what is now and shall be. I attune myself with all that is good for me, so that I will choose wisely. I AM.

Meditation #2.

I affirm that I love everything and everyone. There are things and people that are not easy to love. I will consider the hidden potential for goodness within these things and people—neither actively loving or hating—just being and allowing to be.

There are things I cannot approach, and people I cannot embrace. This is because certain situations present unnecessary burdens and potential danger. But love reaches out afar, as well as embraces near. Love sees the beauty in ugliness and the light within the darkness. Love is free, and liberates all.

I am that I am. Therefore, I love through the Divine Awareness of my being, born of love through Universal Mind. I AM.

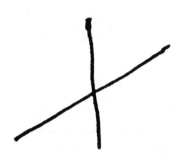

Meditation #3.

I affirm that I am a success in all I think and do. All that occurs in my outer life of everyday awareness is the result of energy from within. Thought is the inner power or energy that creates outward realities.

I will not judge the present or fear the future, based on past failures. I create a new today, and this shall form beautiful tomorrows. I am that I am. My mind is part of the Universal Mind by which all things come into being.

No matter the situation or the lesson of my life, I will look for the positive. I will see the light in the darkness, pleasure in the pain, hope in the hopeless, and life in death. I AM.

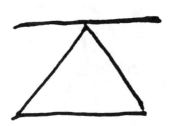

Meditation #4.

I release the painful memories of past mistakes. I ask forgiveness of all people I have harmed, in what I have done or failed to do. I release and forgive all cosmic debts, from past lives as well as my present life.

I will not allow those who hate me to harm me—they can only harm me if I hate them back. Although I cannot associate with some, I release them and love them from afar.

I am that I am. The God/Goddess in me is at peace with all beings in all dimensions. I live and let live in my thoughts, words and deeds. I AM.

Meditation #5.

I affirm that miracle-working cosmic energy flows through me, every moment of my life. I am one with agencies and intelligences in all dimensions, and these powers are ever ready to work in my behalf.

I acknowledge that miracles happen every day: the course of the heavenly bodies, the blooming of the flowers, the cry of a newborn child. All of these are daily miracles. Therefore, I shall expect miracles of health, wealth, and happiness to occur within my life's experience, for I am a channel of miracle energy.

All that I need and desire shall come to me easily, today and every day for the rest of my life. This is so because I allow myself to be guided by Universal Mind. I AM.

The alchemical furnace which enabled the student of the sacred arts to turn metal into gold, as well as transcend time and space.

NOW AVAILABLE FOR THE FIRST TIME!!!

Count St. Germain's IMMORTALITY KIT

YOU CAN BECOME AN ALCHEMIST!
Count Saint Germain—The Most Mysterious Man Of All Ages—Would Like To Share The Secret Of Eternal Youth With You! Secret Formulas Of The World's Greatest Alchemist Revealed For The First Time!!

AMAZING REVELATIONS GUARANTEED TO CHANGE YOUR LIFE

Here is a small sample of what you can expect to learn from the pages of this important manual:

- St. Germain's personal "Purification Ritual."
- His philosophy for an easy and extended life.
- Ridding the body of the "death hormone" which plagues us all.
- Removing the will to die from our subconscious.
- Relaxation, meditation, deep breathing and diet can keep you young.
- Role of mind in overcoming the stigma of death.
- How we go about killing ourselves slowly every day.
- Humankind's spiritual transformation-important plus for New Age.
- Role of Flying Saucers, Angelic Kingdom and Great Brotherhood.
- "Second Coming" part of the "Great Plan."
- Saint Germain and the Great Seal of the United States.
- Famous lives he influenced.
- Secret Societies Saint Germain belonged to.
- Miracles he performed and how they were accomplished.
- Photo of his "digestive furnace" used to create gold and diamonds.
- A letter in his own handwriting.
- Where is he is now and how you can "speak" with him.
- Modern time machine you can enter.

GET THE COMPLETE COUNT SAINT GERMAIN

SECRET INGREDIENT "IMMORTALITY KIT"

AVAILABLE FOR THE FIRST TIME (based on the alchemist's personal mixture)

The Immortality Formula includes St. Germain's little-known "Elixir of Life" which is said to have been used to overcome human limitations to attain immortality.

In Wm Oribello's book you will discover the powerful symbols of immortality and how they are used to transform and guide us to spiritual liberation. Overcome all negativity!

You've read the book...Now order the IMMORTALITY KIT-- $29.95 plus $5 p/h

From: Inner Light
Box 753
New Brunswick, NJ 08903
credit cards 732 602-3407